Science Fair Projects and Activities

Creative Ideas Using Easy-to-Find Materials

WRITTEN BY

Kathleen McFarren and Mike Graf

ILLUSTRATED BY

Diane Valko and Corbin Hillam

2005 • THE LEARNING WORKS

The Learning Works

Editor: Pam VanBlaricum

Illustration: Diane Valko and Corbin Hillam

Book Design: Acorn Studio Books

Art Director: Tom Cochrane

Cover Design: Barbara Peterson

Cover Illustration: Gary Ciccarelli

Project Director: Linda Schwartz

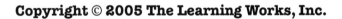

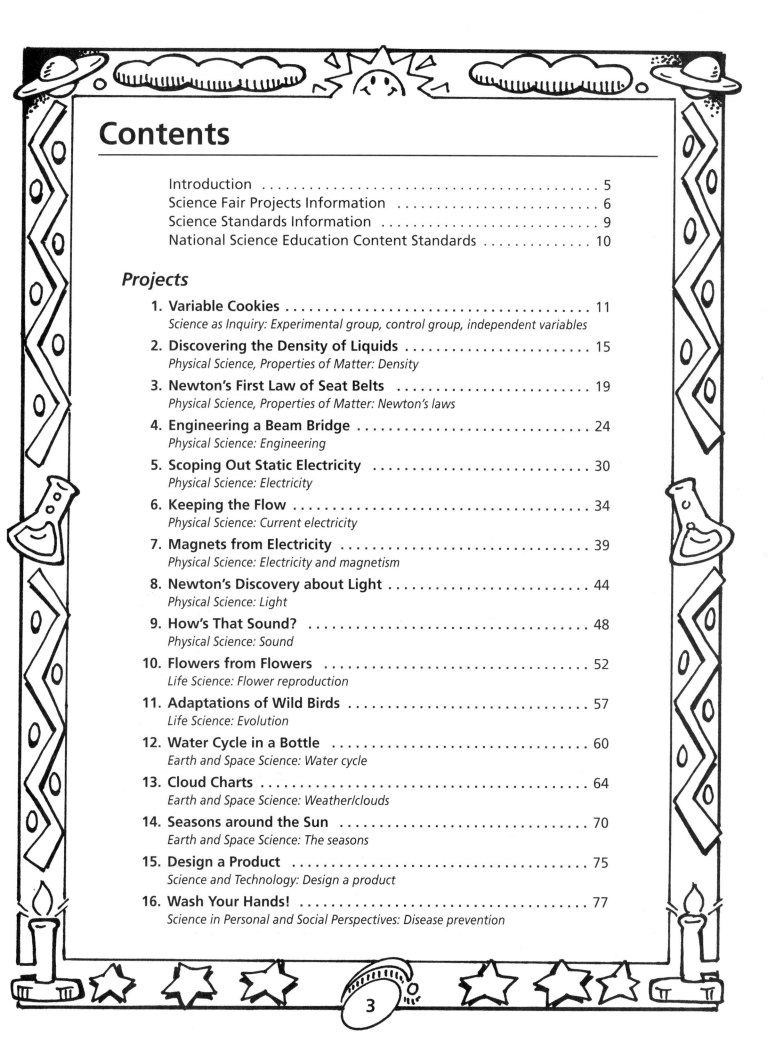

Contents

Projects

Activities

Introduction

Why should you wear a seat belt? What's the best design for a model bridge? Does sound travel best through a gas, a liquid, or a solid? Can clouds help forecast the weather? These are some of the questions that students in grades 5 through 8 will explore while working on the science fair projects presented in this book.

In addition to the science fair projects, hands-on activities are also provided as a way for students to explore such topics as molecules, the electromagnetic spectrum, composting, volcanoes, and the solar system.

All the projects and activities in this book are easy, fun, and interesting. The materials needed to do the projects and activities are inexpensive, and most of the materials can be found at school or at home. The science fair projects follow the guidelines of the scientific method.

In a classroom setting, teachers can assign one project or activity to each student. Or a group of students can work together on a single project or activity. Several students can also work separately on the same project or activity, and then come together at the end to compare their results.

The projects and activities in *Science Fair Projects and Activities* correlate to the National Science Education Standards. According to the NSES Web site, the Standards "outline what students need to know, understand, and be able to do to be scientifically literate at different grade levels." The Web site states that "Schools that implement the Standards will have students learning science by actively engaging in inquiries that are interesting and important to them. Students thereby will establish a knowledge base for understanding science." *Science Fair Projects and Activities* will help satisfy this goal.

Science Fair Projects Information

The Scientific Method

When scientists do experiments, they follow the steps of the scientific method. The scientific method is an orderly way to study a topic of science. You can use the scientific method when you work on your own science fair project. Here are the steps.

1. **Ask a question.** What do you want to know? Write it as a question. Be specific.

2. **Research the topic.** Learn about your topic. Sources of information can be books, magazines, journals, encyclopedias, the Internet, and experts or people knowledgeable about the topics. Each project in this book also includes information. Keep a record of the sources you use so you can write up a bibliography.

3. **Formulate a hypothesis.** The hypothesis answers your question. You write the hypothesis before doing your experiment, so the hypothesis is your best guess of what you think the results will be. When you do the experiment, you're checking to see if your hypothesis is correct.

4. **Plan the experiment.**
   A. Materials
      List the materials you will use in your experiment.
   B. Procedure
      List the steps you will follow.

5. **Do the experiment.** Follow your plan. While you do the experiment, keep notes on what you do, including things you observe and discover. You can record information on tables. You can also create graphs and illustrations, and take photographs.

6. **Write the conclusion.** Summarize what happened during your experiment. Was your hypothesis correct? Why or why not? What did you learn? What would you do differently if you did the experiment again?

7. **Share your findings.** Like all scientists, you should share your findings with other people.

To do this for a science fair, you usually make a science project display. The display shows what you have learned from doing your experiment. Check the rules for your own school's science fair to find out the exact requirements for your display. One idea is shown on the following page.

Sample project using the scientific method

1. **Ask a question.** Does land or water heat up faster?

2. **Research the topic.** I studied three books about water and the ocean. I also talked to a science teacher.

3. **Formulate a hypothesis.** The land will heat up faster.

4. **Plan the experiment.**
   A. Materials
      two plastic cups
      water
      dirt
      freezer
      two thermometers

B. Procedure

1. Fill one cup with water.

2. Fill the other cup with dirt.

3. Place the cups in the freezer for 20 minutes. By first starting with cold water and cold dirt in this experiment, it is easier to see a change in temperature when the water and the dirt warm up in the sun.

4. Remove the cups from the freezer. Put a thermometer into the cup of water. Push another thermometer down into the cup of soil. Wait two minutes before reading the temperatures on each thermometer. Write down these temperatures.

5. Leave the thermometers in the cups and place the cups outside in bright sunlight for 20 minutes. Write down these temperatures.

5. **Do the experiment.** As I followed the procedure, I recorded the temperatures in a table. The results are shown below.

Sample	Temperature after freezer	Temperature after sunshine
Water	13°C (55°F)	26°C (79°F)
Dirt	14°C (57°F)	33°C (91°F)

6. **Write the conclusion.** The water warmed up by just 13°C after being in the sun. But the dirt warmed up by 19°C . The dirt represented land. This means that land warms up sooner than water. My hypothesis was correct. If I did the experiment again, I would fill a third cup with salt water. That way, I can compare the temperatures of ocean water with fresh water.

7. **Share your findings.** I made a display for the science fair. In front of the display, I set out the cup of water and the cup of dirt with the thermometers inside both cups.

Create your own science fair project following the scientific method. You can also try one of the sixteen science fair projects in this book.

Science Activities Information

This book also contains fourteen science activities. Each activity lets you explore one topic of science.

Science Standards Information

The national standards for science are called the National Science Education Standards (NSES). According to the NSES Web site, the standards "are designed to guide our nation toward a scientifically literate society. Founded in exemplary practice and research, the Standards describe a vision of the scientifically literate person and present criteria for science education that will allow that vision to become reality." The site goes on to explain that "The Standards rest on the premise that science is an active process. Science is something that students do, not something that is done to them."

The NSES for grades 5 through 8 are divided into seven different Science Content Standards as shown below.

- Content Standard A: Science as Inquiry

- Content Standard B: Physical Science

- Content Standard C: Life Science

- Content Standard D: Earth and Space Science

- Content Standard E: Science and Technology

- Content Standard F: Science in Personal and Social Perspectives

- Content Standard G: History and Nature of Science

The science fair projects and activities in this book are based on the Standards. There is at least one project or activity for each of the Content Standards A through G. The table on page 10 compares the standards addressed by the various projects and activities.

The NSES Web site can be found at www.nap.edu/readingroom/books/nses/html.

National Science Education Content Standards

Project	Content Standard	Category
1. Variable Cookies	A. Science as Inquiry	Scientific Investigation
2. Discovering the Density of Liquids	B. Physical Science	Properties of Matter
3. Newton's First Law of Seat Belts	B. Physical Science	Motion & Force
4. Engineering a Beam Bridge	B. Physical Science	Motion & Force
5. Scoping Out Static Electricity	B. Physical Science	Energy
6. Keeping the Flow	B. Physical Science	Energy
7. Magnets from Electricity	B. Physical Science	Energy
8. Newton's Discovery about Light	B. Physical Science	Energy
9. How's That Sound?	B. Physical Science	Energy
10. Flowers from Flowers	C. Life Science	Reproduction
11. Adaptations of Wild Birds	C. Life Science	Regulation & Behavior
12. Water Cycle in a Bottle	D. Earth & Space Science	Structure of the Earth System
13. Cloud Charts	D. Earth & Space Science	Structure of the Earth System
14. Seasons around the Sun	D. Earth & Space Science	Structure of the Earth System
15. Design a Project	E. Science & Technology	Technological Design
16. Wash Your Hands!	F. Personal & Social Perspectives	Personal Health
17. Build a Periodic Table of the Elements	B. Physical Science	Properties of Matter
18. Gumdrop Molecules	B. Physical Science	Properties of Matter
19. Presto Change-O Water	B. Physical Science	Properties of Matter
20. Touring the Electromagnetic Spectrum	B. Physical Science	Energy
21. Plant and Animal Cells	C. Life Science	Living Systems
22. Compost Jug	C. Life Science	Populations & Ecosystems
23. Endangered Species Posters	C. Life Science	Diversity & Adaptation
24. Puzzling Plates	D. Earth & Space Science	Structure of the Earth System
25. Three Erupting Volcanoes	D. Earth & Space Science	Structure of the Earth System
26. Recycled Rocks	D. Earth & Space Science	Structure of the Earth System
27. Wind Watching	D. Earth & Space Science	Structure of the Earth System
28. Geologic Time Scale	D. Earth & Space Science	Earth's History
29. Our Solar System	D. Earth & Space Science	Earth in Solar System
30. Moon Tracker	D. Earth & Space Science	Earth in Solar System

CATEGORY: Science as Inquiry
TOPIC: Experimental group, control group, and independent variables

Project 1:
Variable Cookies

National Science Education Standards: Science as Inquiry, Content Standard A: Design and Conduct a Scientific Investigation ("Students should develop general abilities, such as systematic observation, making accurate measurements, and identifying and controlling variables.")

Introduction

With this project, you use a scientific testing technique while experimenting with a chocolate chip cookie recipe.

Experiment

1. **Ask a question.** What happens when you bake several batches of chocolate chip cookies and you leave out a different ingredient in each batch?

2. **Research the topic.** See Information Sources.

3. **Formulate a hypothesis.** What do you think? (Write your own hypothesis.)

4. **Plan the experiment.**
   ### A. Materials
masking tape	*Total cookie ingredients for all batches—*
pen	2 cups butter or margarine
seven small mixing bowls	2 cups white granulated sugar
measuring spoons	2 cups brown sugar
measuring cups	3 whole eggs
mixing spoon	6 cups flour
two small spoons	3 teaspoons baking soda
cookie sheets	2⅓ cups chocolate chips
oil or cooking spray	
oven	
hot pads	
plastic bags	

> ### * Information Sources
> Visit your library and find books about the scientific method. One suggested book is *Guide to the Best Science Fair Projects* by Janice VanCleave (New York: John Wiley and Sons, Inc., 1997). You can search the Internet by typing in this keyword: the scientific method. Also read the Background Information about scientific experiments on page 14 of this book.

B. Procedure

1. Tear or cut off seven pieces of masking tape. With the pen, number the tape pieces 1 through 7. These are the batch numbers. Next to each batch number on the tape, write in the missing ingredient. For batch 1, write "All ingredients." Tape one number to each of the seven mixing bowls. Note: For each batch, you will use only those ingredients and amounts shown on the table below for that particular batch. Batch 1 contains all the ingredients. This is the control group. Each of the remaining batches is missing one ingredient. These batches are the experimental groups. The missing ingredient is the independent variable. Since you're making chocolate chip cookies, all the batches will have chocolate chips.

Batch #	Butter	White Sugar	Brown Sugar	Eggs	Flour	Baking Soda	Chips
1	1/3 cup	1/3 cup	1/3 cup	1/2 egg	1 cup	1/2 teaspoon	1/3 cup
2	———	1/3 cup	1/3 cup	1/2 egg	1 cup	1/2 teaspoon	1/3 cup
3	1/3 cup	———	1/3 cup	1/2 egg	1 cup	1/2 teaspoon	1/3 cup
4	1/3 cup	1/3 cup	———	1/2 egg	1 cup	1/2 teaspoon	1/3 cup
5	1/3 cup	1/3 cup	1/3 cup	———	1 cup	1/2 teaspoon	1/3 cup
6	1/3 cup	1/3 cup	1/3 cup	1/2 egg	———	1/2 teaspoon	1/3 cup
7	1/3 cup	1/3 cup	1/3 cup	1/2 egg	1 cup	———	1/3 cup
Total	2 cups	2 cups	2 cups	3 eggs	6 cups	3 teaspoons	2-1/3 cups

BATCH #3

2. Prepare the cookie dough for each batch. For the first batch, thoroughly mix together the butter, white sugar, brown sugar, and egg. Then mix in the flour and baking soda. Finally, stir in the chocolate chips. Do the same for the other batches, but leave out the one ingredient for that batch.

3. Grease a cookie sheet. Spoon lumps of batter from just one bowl onto the cookie sheet. Bake the cookies at 375°F for about 12 minutes. Remove the cookies from the oven and let cool. Set the empty bowl with the batch number still on it by the cookie sheet to help you identify which batch of cookies it is. When the cookies are cool, place them in a plastic bag. Remove the masking tape label from the bowl and put it on the plastic bag. Wash the cookie sheet.

4. Repeat Steps 2 and 3 for each batch of cookie dough.

5. Check each batch of cookies for appearance and taste. You might ask other people to also do a taste test on the different batches.

5. **Do the experiment.** While you do the experiment, keep notes on what you do, including things you observe and discover. Record the results of your experiment on a table like the one shown below.

Batch #	Type of Group (check one)		Independent variable (write the missing ingredient)	Appearance	Taste
	Control	Experimental			
1			none		
2			butter		
3			white sugar		
4			brown sugar		
5			egg		
6			flour		
7			baking soda		

6. **Write the conclusion.** Summarize what happened during the experiment. How did the independent variables affect the cookies' appearance and taste for each batch? Did some independent variables affect the cookies more than others? How does the experimental group compare to the control group of cookies? What would you do differently if you did the experiment again?

7. **Share your findings.** Create a science project display to show what you have learned from doing your experiment. Check the rules for your own school's science fair to find out the exact requirements for your display. An idea for a display is on page 7.

Background Information: Scientific Experiments

You already know that scientists use the scientific method to do experiments. They ask a question, research the topic, formulate a hypothesis, plan the experiment, do the experiment, write a conclusion, and share their findings.

Scientists also follow a special procedure when they test something during an experiment. This procedure helps make sure their results are as accurate as possible.

Let's say the scientist wants to test different fertilizers on some bean plants. The group of bean plants she will test is called the experimental group. The bean plants are all the same kind and size. The bean plants are also grown in the same size pot, with the same type of soil, and with the same amount of sunlight. That way, the scientist can compare just the effects of the fertilizers on the plants.

The thing that the scientist changes each time during an experiment is called the independent variable. In this case, the independent variable is the type of fertilizer. There is usually only one independent variable per test. This means the scientist knows that it is the thing that caused the changes to the experimental group.

While the scientist is testing the experimental group, she also has a control group. The control group doesn't use the independent variable. That way, she can see how the test objects would do without any changes. For the fertilizer experiment, the control group would be bean plants that get no fertilizer. The scientist can see how the control group of bean plants does without any fertilizer and compare it to the experimental group.

Extension

With this project, you tested chocolate chip cookies. Try setting up your own experiment with some other experimental group, control group, and independent variable. You might try a different cookie recipe, or use a recipe for a different kind of food. Or perhaps you'd like to try testing fertilizers on bean plants. What else would you like to test?

Category: Physical Science: Properties of Matter
Topic: Density

Project 2:
Discovering the
Density of Liquids

National Science Education Standards: Physical Science, Content Standard B: Properties and Changes of Properties in Matter ("A substance has characteristic properties, such as density...")

Introduction

With this project, you will measure the density of different liquids.

Experiment

1. **Ask a question.** Is water more or less dense than salt water, alcohol, vegetable oil, and pancake syrup?

2. **Research the topic.** See Information Sources.

3. **Formulate a hypothesis.** The density of water is greater than the density of alcohol, but less than the density of salt water, vegetable oil, and pancake syrup.

4. **Plan the experiment.**
   A. Materials
   five 10-ounce (296 ml) clear plastic disposable drinking cups
   measuring cup
   ¾ cup drinking water
   ¾ cup salt water (dissolve 3 tablespoons of salt in ¾ cup of water)
   ¾ cup vegetable oil
   ¾ cup rubbing alcohol
   ¾ cup pancake syrup
   drinking straws
   scissors
   modeling clay
   ruler
   laundry marker

* Information Sources

Visit your library and find books about density. One suggested book is *The Way Science Works* by Robin Kerrod and Sharon Ann Holgate (New York: DK Publishing, Inc., 2002). You can search the Internet by typing in these keywords: hydrometer, relative density, and specific gravity. Also read the Background Information about density on page 18 of this book.

B. Procedure

1. Make hydrometers to measure the density of the liquids. To make one, cut a straw into a 2-inch length. Push a small ball of modeling clay onto one end of the straw. Repeat to make four more hydrometers.

2. Because the hydrometers will be slightly different from one another, calibrate them to the density level of water. On one of the hydrometers, use the laundry marker to draw dots at ⅛ inch increments up the side of the straw from the top of the clay ball to the tip of the straw. Let the ink dots dry for about 10 minutes. Fill one of the plastic cups with ¾ cup of drinking water. Float the marked hydrometer, clay side down, in the water. Bend down and look through the side of the cup. Notice where the surface level of the water comes in relation to the dots you drew on the straw. Pull the hydrometer out of the water and mark the surface level of the water by drawing a ring all the way around the straw. This shows the density level of the water. Repeat this step to calibrate the other four hydrometers.

3. Use the hydrometers to measure the relative densities of the salt water, vegetable oil, rubbing alcohol, and pancake syrup. Set out the four remaining cups. Put ¾ cup of drinking water in the first cup, ¾ cup of salt water in the second cup, ¾ cup of vegetable oil in the third cup, ¾ cup of rubbing alcohol in the fourth cup, and ¾ cup of pancake syrup in the fifth cup. Let the cups sit for ten minutes so that the liquids are about the same temperature. After the ten minutes, set a hydrometer in each of the liquids. Bend down and look through the side of the cup. Compare the heights of the different hydrometers as they float in the liquids. Also look at the markings you made on the hydrometers. Denser liquids push the hydrometer up higher, so the mark on the straw will be above the surface of the liquid. In less dense liquids, the straw sinks down farther, so the mark on the straw is lower than the surface of the liquid. Do any of the liquids have the same density as water?

5. Do the experiment. While you do the experiment, keep notes on what you do, including things you observe and discover. List the liquids, including the drinking water, in order from the least dense to the most dense. Make a list like the one shown below.

Liquids in order of density (in ascending order, least dense first)

1. _____

2. _____

3. _____

4. _____

5. _____

---

6. Write the conclusion. Summarize what happened during the experiment. What did you find out about the densities of the different liquids? What would you do differently if you did the experiment again?

7. Share your findings. Create a science project display to show what you have learned from doing your experiment. Check the rules for your own school's science fair to find out the exact requirements for your display. An idea for a display is on page 7.

Background Information: Density

Density is a measure of the number of objects contained in a certain volume of space. The more objects there are in the space, the greater the density. Imagine filling two clear plastic cubes that are the same size with marbles. In one cube, you put just 5 marbles. In the other cube, you put 50. The second cube has a greater density than the first because it contains more objects in the same amount of space.

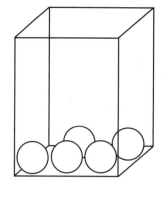
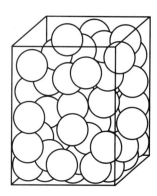

Density is also a measure of how much matter there is in a certain volume of liquid such as oil or water. The matter can be atoms, molecules, and other particles like salt or sugar. The more matter there is in the substance, the denser the substance tends to be.

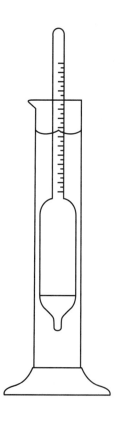

The temperature of a substance also affects density. In a warm substance, the molecules are farther apart. This means the substance is less dense. If that same volume of substance becomes cold, the molecules move closer together. This means the substance is denser. Warm water is less dense than cold water, and warm air is less dense than cold air.

A floating instrument called a hydrometer is used to measure the density of liquids. It floats higher in denser liquids than in less dense liquids. That's because there is more matter in a dense liquid to push up the hydrometer. A less dense liquid provides a smaller push upward, so the hydrometer floats lower in the water.

The hydrometer measures the relative density of a particular substance. This means that the density of the substance is compared to the density of the same volume of water. The relative density of water is 1. If the substance has a relative density less than 1, it is less dense than water. If its relative density is greater than 1, it is denser than water.

Extension

Find out what the Plimsoll line is on a ship and what it has to do with the density of water the ship sails in.

Category: Physical Science: Properties of Matter
Topic: Newton's Laws

Project 3:
Newton's First
Law of Seat Belts

National Science Education Standards: Physical Science, Content Standard B: Motions and Forces ("An object that is not being subjected to a force will continue to move at a constant speed and in a straight line.")

Introduction

With this project, you'll explore Newton's First Law of Motion and see what it has to do with wearing seat belts.

Experiment

1. **Ask a question.** According to Newton's First Law of Motion, why should you wear a seat belt while riding in an automobile?

2. **Research the topic.** See Information Sources.

3. **Formulate a hypothesis.** If an automobile stops suddenly, Newton's First Law of Motion says that passengers and objects in the car will continue moving at the speed of the car before it stopped. Wearing a seat belt will prevent this movement.

4. **Plan the experiment.**
   A. Materials

   Motion detector—
      empty cardboard cold cereal box
        (about 8" x 12" x 2")
      scissors
      masking tape
      hole punch
      glue
      ping pong ball

   Crash test track—
      two long, hollow tubes about 30"
        long and 2¾" in diameter (tubes
        from rolled gift wrap work well)
      masking tape

   yard stick
   pencil
   one lightweight piece of cardboard
      cut into a rectangle about
      1" high by 4" long
   small toy car (about 1" wide by 2½" long)
   one 10-ounce (296 ml) clear plastic
      disposable drinking cup

   Also—
      cup
      small rock
      stop watch (or wrist watch
        with chronograph)

* Information Sources

Visit your library and find books about safety and seat belts. Two suggested books are *Time-Life Student Library: Physical Science* (Virginia: Time-Life Books, 2000) and *Eyewitness Science: Force and Motion* by Peter Lafferty (New York: Dorling Kindersley, Inc., 1992). You can search the Internet by typing in these keywords: Newton's Laws of Motion, and seat belt safety. Also read the Background Information about Newton's first law on page 23 of this book.

B. Procedure

Motion detector—

1. Cut out the front side of the cereal box, leaving a ¼ inch border all the way around to make a frame. Tape the flaps closed at the top of the box. Cut out a 1" square from the piece of cardboard you cut from the front of the box. Use a hole punch to punch a hole in the middle of the square. Lay the box down flat on a table, with the cut-out front facing up. Tape the square to the center of the bottom of the box. It will be a stand to hold the ball in place until the car starts moving.

2. Next time you're riding in a car or bus, set the motion detector box flat on the floor near you. The shorter edges should face the front and back of the vehicle. Secure the box so it won't move while the car or bus is in motion. Place the ping-pong ball on the punched square in the middle of the box. As the vehicle moves, watch the ball. How often does it stay still? How often does it move? In which direction does it roll when the car stops, accelerates, turns left, and turns right? What forces cause the ball to move as it does? Compare the motion of the ball to the motion of your body. Take the motion detector with you on several different car trips.

Crash test track—

1. Make the test track. Cut one cardboard tube in half lengthwise. Put one half inside the other to make a strong half-pipe track. Repeat with the other tube. Put the two tube sections together end-to-end, overlapping them about 1 inch. Tape the tube sections together to make one half-pipe track that is about 60 inches long. Lay the half-pipe track on the floor with the long, cut edges facing upward. Tape both ends of the track to the floor so it won't slide around.

2. Make a crash wall for the end of the track. Cut ½-inch-long by ⅛ inch wide slots on both sides of the track, about 1" in from one end of the track. Slide the 1" by 4" piece of cardboard into the pair of slots to make the crash wall. Tape the crash wall to the track.

3. Make a "car seat" for the test vehicle's passenger. Shorten the plastic cup by cutting off about 2 inches from the top of it. Set the cup on its side on the roof of the toy car, with the open end of the cup facing forward. Tape the cup to the roof so that the front of the cup tips slightly upward. Place the rock, which will be the passenger, toward the back of the cup. If the rock falls out, tip the front of the cup up a bit more and tape the cup in this position.

4. Set the car on the track at the opposite end from the crash wall so that it faces the crash wall. The back wheels of the car should be just inside the edge of the track. Use the yard stick to measure the distance from the front wheels of the car to the crash wall, and write down this measurement. You will use this same distance when determining the different speeds of the car.

5. Lay the yard stick along one side of the track so it is parallel to the track. Slide the yard stick down so that its zero end lines up with the crash wall. The other end of the yard stick should be facing away from the track. Tape the yard stick down. This will be used to measure the distance the passenger (rock) is thrown from the vehicle.

6. Now you'll do three different crash tests at different speeds. For Test #1, use only a little force to push the car down the track so that it just reaches the crash wall. First, predict what you think will happen to the passenger (rock). Then do the experiment. Have a helper use the stop watch to keep track of how long it takes the car to reach the crash wall. Write down this time. Check the yard stick to see what distance, if any, the passenger was thrown after the car stopped at the crash wall. Write down this distance. Are the results what you predicted? What caused the passenger to keep moving, even though the car stopped? Newton's First Law states that a moving object will continue moving in a straight line at the same speed until a force acts on it. No force acted to hold the passenger in place, so it kept moving.

7. For Test #2, use more force to push the car down the track to the crash wall. First predict what you think will happen at this greater speed. Then do the experiment, writing down the time it took for the car to reach the crash wall and the distance the passenger was thrown. Was your prediction right this time?

8. For Test #3, repeat Test #2, but this time use a lot of force to push the car.

9. For Test #4, fashion some masking tape into a seat belt and secure the passenger (rock) into the plastic cup seat. Use a lot of force to push the car down the track. What happens to the passenger this time? What force keeps the passenger in the seat?

5. **Do the experiment.** While you do the experiment, keep notes on what you do, including things you observe and discover. Record the results of your crash tests on a table like the one shown below. To find the speed the vehicle was going for each trial run, divide the distance (in inches) by the time. For example, if the distance is 57 inches and the time is 3 seconds, the speed is 19 inches per second. If the distance is 57 inches and the time is 2.2 seconds, the speed is 25.91 inches per second.

Test #	Seat belts		Distance car traveled	Time elapsed	Speed (distance ÷ time)	Distance passenger thrown
	Yes	No				
1						
2						
3						
4						

6. **Write the conclusion.** Summarize what happened during the experiment. What did you find out by using the motion detector while riding in a vehicle? What did you find out by doing the crash test? How did the speed of the car affect how far the passenger (rock) was thrown from the car? What would you do differently if you did the experiment again?

7. **Share your findings.** Create a science project display to show what you have learned from doing your experiment. Check the rules for your own school's science fair to find out the exact requirements for your display. An idea for a display is on page 7.

Background Information: Newton's First Law of Motion

Isaac Newton was an English scientist from the 1600s. He discovered scientific laws about forces and moving objects.

A force is something that changes the way an object moves. It can speed up the object, slow it down, or make it change direction. There are many kinds of forces that can act on objects, but all objects on Earth experience the force of gravity and friction. Gravity is the attractive force that Earth has on objects. Friction is a force that is created by two objects rubbing together.

Newton's First Law of Motion states that an object sitting still will not move unless some force acts on it. If a car is sitting in a parking lot, it won't move unless the force of the engine moves it. Newton's First Law also states that a moving object will continue moving in a straight line at the same speed until a force acts on it. A moving car traveling north down a highway at 60 miles per hour will continue doing so until the driver presses the accelerator pedal, applies the brakes, or steers the car in a different direction.

Newton's First Law also applies to passengers in automobiles. While a car is speeding down a highway, the passengers inside are swept along at the same speed and in the same direction as the car. If the car suddenly stops, the passengers continue traveling at the same speed as the car had been going. If the car was going 20 miles per hour, the passengers will continue moving at that speed. If the car was speeding along at 60 miles per hour, so will the passengers.

According to Newton's First Law, the passengers will continue moving through the car after a sudden stop unless some force stops them. If the passengers are wearing seat belts, the force of the belt will hold them in place. If they are not wearing seat belts, they can try to hold on to something inside the car. If the car was traveling at a great enough speed, though, the passengers continue to move so rapidly through the car that they don't usually have the time or the strength to grab on to something. Instead they are often thrown into the dashboard or windshield—or worse, ejected completely from the car.

Extension

Find out what happens when you vary the mass of the passenger (rock) with the crash test track.

Category: Physical Science
Topic: Engineering

Project 4:
Engineering a Beam Bridge

National Science Education Standards: Physical Sciences, Content Standard B: Motions and Forces ("If more than one force acts on an object...then the forces will reinforce or cancel one another..."). Content Standard F: Abilities of Technological Design, Design a solution or product ("Students should make and compare different proposals in light of the criteria they have selected. They must...communicate ideas with drawings and simple models.")

Introduction

With this project, you design and build a model bridge that is strong enough to support a golf ball. Invite other people to do this same project so you can compare your bridge designs.

Experiment

1. **Ask a question.** What is the best design for a model beam bridge that meets all the criteria described in the Background Information?

2. **Research the topic.** See Information Sources.

3. **Formulate a hypothesis.** What do you think? Write your own hypothesis to answer the question.

4. **Plan the experiment.**
   A. Materials
      Materials for one model beam bridge—
         five sheets of 9" x 12" construction paper, any color
         scissors
         glue
         optional: one photocopy of the shape pattern (cube, rectangular box, and triangular prism, page 25), enlarged to whatever size you wish

      Test weight for the model beam bridge—
         one standard golf ball
         one piece of clear tape

*Information Sources

Visit your library and find books about engineering and bridges. One suggested book is *Time-Life Student Library: Physical Sciences* (Virginia: Time-Life Books, 2000). You can search the Internet by typing in these keywords: bridges and engineers. Check out bridge information on the "How Stuff Works" Web site at travel.howstuffworks.com/bridge1. Also read the Background Information about engineers and bridges on pages 28–29 of this book.

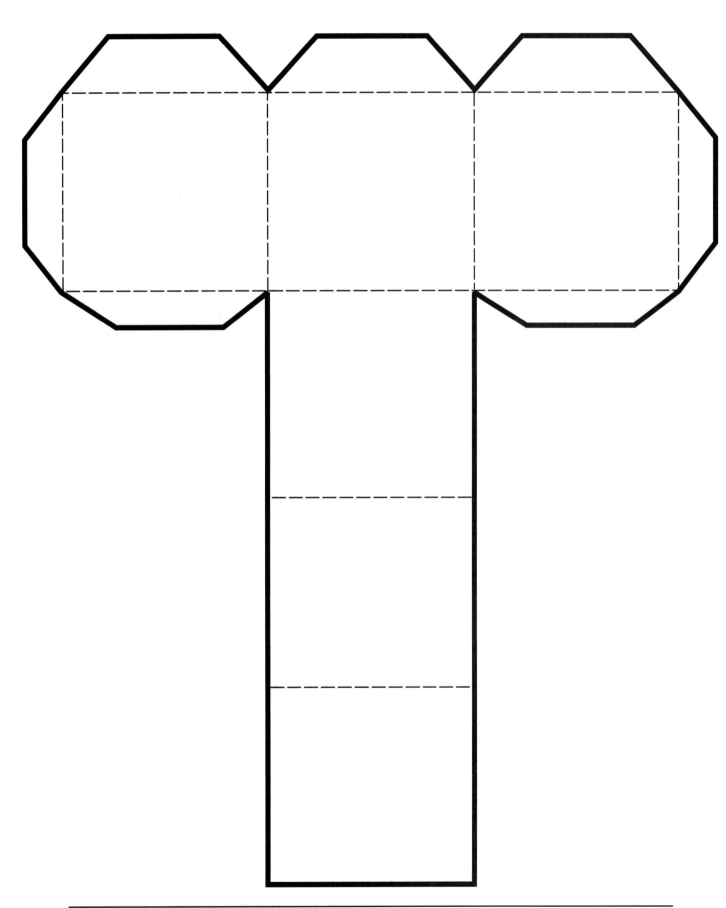

B. Procedure

1. Use 5 sheets of construction paper, scissors, and glue to build a model of a beam bridge. You can use the pattern to make cubes, rectangular prisms, and triangular prisms from the construction paper for any bridge parts. Make as many models as you wish.

5. Do the experiment. While you do the experiment, keep notes on what you do, including things you observe and discover. Record information about your model bridge prototypes on a table like the one below. Be sure to keep all your sketches and model bridges with the information in the table. The sketches, models, and table form a complete account of your work on beam bridges.

Prototype #	Is a beam bridge		Supported by two piers made of construction paper		Made of 5 or fewer sheets of construction paper and glue		Span between piers = 10"		Supports a golf ball taped in the exact center		Entire span 2" or higher above table with ball in place	
	Yes	No	Yes	No	Yes	No	Yes	No	Yes	No	Yes	No
1												
2												
3												
4												

6. Write the conclusion. Summarize what happened during the experiment. How many different prototypes of model bridges did you make? What was your best design and why? Were you successful in meeting all the criteria for making your model bridge? What would you do differently if you did the project again?

7. Share your findings. Create a science project display to show what you have learned from doing your experiment. Check the rules for your own school's science fair to find out the exact requirements for your display. An idea for a display is on page 7. Display your most successful model bridge as well as one or two of the prototypes.

Background Information: Engineers and Bridges

Engineers are people who are trained to design and build many different things, including machines, electrical equipment, and structures such as buildings, roads, and bridges.

When engineers design bridges, they use science and math to figure out all the forces that could act on the bridge. A force is a pull or a push on an object. A force that pulls or stretches something apart is called tension. A force that pushes or squeezes something together is called compression. For example, a wire spring experiences tension when you stretch it out and compression when you let it go back together.

All bridges experience tension and compression. These forces can act horizontally, vertically, and diagonally. When one part of a bridge experiences tension, another part experiences compression. Tension and compression forces acting on a bridge can be caused by many things, including gravity, the weight and movement of traffic, temperature, wind, and earthquakes. The engineer's job is to design the bridge so that it can handle all the forces without breaking apart and collapsing.

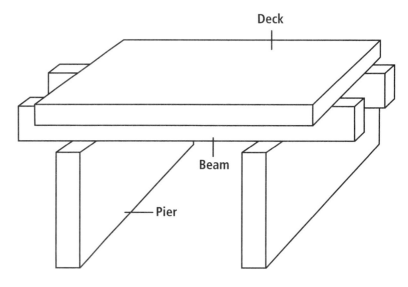

There are many different kinds of bridges. The beam bridge is one of the oldest and simplest styles. It has horizontal beams that rest on supports called piers. The deck is the platform that supports the traffic. The deck can be above the beams, below the beams, or in between two beams.

As the weight of the traffic, deck, and beam pushes down on the piers of a beam bridge, the beams tend to bend downward. The bottom of the beam stretches apart, so it experiences tension. At the same time, the top of the beam squeezes together, so it experiences compression.

When engineers design bridges, they must work within certain given criteria. These criteria include how far the bridge must span, how much traffic the bridge must support, what materials are available to build the bridge, and how much money they can spend.

For this project, your job is to build a model beam bridge. It must meet the following criteria: 1) it must be a beam bridge, with a deck, beams, and piers; 2) it must be held up on two construction paper piers of any shape; 3) the bridge and the two piers must be constructed out of no more than five sheets of construction paper and glue; 4) the span (distance) between the two piers (from the inside face of one pier to the inside face of the second pier) must be exactly 10 inches;

5) the deck and beams must be strong enough to support the weight of a standard golf ball taped to the exact middle of the span; and 6) while the golf ball rests on the bridge, the bottom of the lower horizontal surface of the span (the beam or the deck—whichever is lower) must be 2 inches or more above the surface on which the model bridge stands.

For your paper bridge, the paper can be cut, folded, and/or glued into different shapes to make the parts of the bridge. Try making the piers from square or rectangular prisms, tubes, or even cones. Beams can be round tubes, square tubes, or shaped like the letter "I," called an I-beam. The deck can be flat, a thin box shape, or folded like a fan. What other design ideas can you think of for each of the bridge parts?

Extension

Find out about the many other types of bridges, including fixed bridges and moveable bridges. What kinds of bridges are there where you live? How are they put together? Why do you think the engineer who designed each bridge chose that particular type?

Category: Physical Science
Topic: Static Electricity

Project 5:
Scoping Out Static Electricity

National Science Education Standards: Physical Science, Content Standard B: Transfer of Energy ("Energy is a property of many substances and is associated with...electricity..." and "Electrical circuits provide a means of transferring electrical energy.")

Introduction

With this project, you will test objects to see if they have static electricity.

Experiment

1. **Ask a question.** How does an electroscope show that an object has static electricity?

2. **Research the topic.** See Information Sources.

3. **Formulate a hypothesis.** The tips of the foil strips on the electroscope move apart when an object with static electricity touches the electroscope.

4. **Plan the experiment.**
   A. Materials
   glass jar with a *plastic* lid
   1 jumbo (1¾" long) paper clip (not plastic-coated)
   1 large, brass paper fastener
   masking tape
   strip of aluminum foil (about ¾" by 3")
   Styrofoam plate, as well as other objects to rub on your hair, such as a comb, a blown-up balloon, a piece of wool, and a sheet of plastic

> **** Information Sources***
> Visit your library and find books about electricity and static electricity. One suggested book is *The Way Science Works* by Robin Kerrod and Sharon Ann Holgate (New York: DK Publishing, Inc., 2002). You can search the Internet by typing in these keywords: electricity and static electricity. Also read the Background Information about static electricity on page 33 of this book.

B. Procedure

1. Make the electroscope. First have an adult poke a small hole in the center of the plastic lid. Straighten out the paper clip and form it into an "L" shape. Push the top end of the paper clip up through the hole in the lid. Tape the paper fastener to the top of the paper clip above the lid. Fold the foil strip in half and drape it over the bottom of the "L." Carefully screw the lid on the jar. The foil strip should not touch the jar.

2. For Test #1, see if the Styrofoam plate already has static electricity before rubbing it on your hair. To do this, simply touch the plate to the paper fastener on the electroscope. What happens to the tips of the foil strips?

3. For Test #2, rub the Styrofoam plate on your hair, and then touch the plate to the paper fastener. What happens to the ends of the foil strips this time?

4. Use your electroscope to test for static electricity on the other objects you selected. Do the first test on the object where you don't rub it on your hair. Then do the second test on the object after you've rubbed it on your hair.

---

5. Do the experiment. While you do the experiment, keep notes on what you do, including things you observe and discover. Record the results of your tests for static electricity on a table like the one shown below.

Test Material	Test #1 Results before rubbing on hair (check one)		Test #2 Results after rubbing on hair (check one)	
	Foil strips don't move apart	Foil strips do move apart	Foil strips don't move apart	Foil strips do move apart
1. Styrofoam plate				
2.				
3.				
4.				
5.				

6. Write the conclusion. Summarize what happened during the experiment. Did your electroscope show whether or not objects have static electricity? Why or why not? What would you do differently if you did the experiment again?

7. Share your findings. Create a science project display to show what you have learned from doing your experiment. Check the rules for your own school's science fair to find out the exact requirements for your display. An idea for a display is on page 7.

Background Information: Static Electricity

All objects are made up of tiny particles called atoms. Inside the atoms are positively-charged protons and negatively-charged electrons. An atom usually contains the same number of electrons as protons. This means the atom is electrically neutral. Objects that contain mostly electrically neutral atoms tend to be electrically neutral. Electrically neutral objects do not have static electricity.

When two electrically neutral objects like a balloon and your hair are rubbed together, electrons are transferred between them. Electrons, rather than protons, are transferred because electrons move around more freely inside the atom. In this case, the balloon gains electrons. Since the balloon's atoms have more electrons than protons, the balloon is negatively charged. At the same time, your hair loses electrons. Your hair's atoms have more protons than electrons, so your hair is positively charged. The balloon and your hair are no longer electrically neutral. Instead, they both have static electricity.

When an object has static electricity, it is attracted to objects that have an opposite charge. The negatively charged balloon is attracted to your positively-charged hair. At the same time, objects with static electricity repel or move away from objects with the same charge. If you put two negatively-charged balloons together, they repel each other.

7 electrons   5 protons

NEGATIVELY CHARGED ATOM

3 electrons   5 protons

POSITIVELY CHARGED ATOM

An object with static electricity can become electrically-neutral once again by rubbing against an object with an opposite charge. That's why objects with opposite charges are attracted to each other. When these objects touch, electrons transfer between them. When the negatively-charged balloon touches your positively-charged hair, electrons transfer from your hair to the balloon. The balloon and your hair no longer have a static electric charge. They are electrically-neutral.

Static means "unmoving." Static electricity doesn't move through wires. Current electricity—which runs computers, radios, and lights—does.

An electroscope is a device that can show whether an object has static electricity. Do this project to find out how it works.

Extension

Lightning happens as a result of static electricity. Find out about it. Why did Benjamin Franklin study lightning, and what did he discover?

Category: Physical Science
Topic: Current Electricity

Project 6:
Keeping the Flow

Information Sources

Visit your library and find books about electricity. One suggested book is *The Way Science Works* by Robin Kerrod and Sharon Ann Holgate (New York: DK Publishing, Inc., 2002). You can search the Internet by typing in these keywords: electricity and conductors. Also read the Background Information about current electricity and conductors on page 38 of this book.

National Science Education Standards: Physical Science, Content Standard B: Transfer of Energy ("Energy is a property of many substances and is associated with…light, electricity…" and "Electrical circuits provide a means of transferring electrical energy.")

Introduction

With this project, you'll set up an electrical circuit to test different materials to see which can carry electricity and which cannot.

Experiment

1. **Ask a question.** What objects are conductors and what objects are insulators?

2. **Research the topic.** See Information Sources.

3. **Formulate a hypothesis.** Objects that are conductors are made of metal, and objects that are insulators are not.

4. **Plan the experiment.**
   A. Materials

   20-gauge insulated electrical wire (bell wire), three feet long
   scissors or wire strippers
   four small alligator clips
   6-volt electric cell (battery)
   small flashlight bulb for 6-volt electric cell and matching bulb holder
   screwdriver
   one hard, dry sponge, or a thick piece of cardboard
   brass paper fasteners (brads)
   one jumbo (1¾" long) paper clip
   5 to 10 objects to test for conductivity, such as paper, plastic, erasers, thread, toothpicks, scissors, crayons, pencils, pens, foil, coins, pennies, rulers, pins, leaves, keys, rubber bands, and leather

B. Procedure

1. Cut the wire into three shorter pieces that are each one foot long. Cut off about ¼" of the plastic coating from both ends of each of the foot-long wires. Be careful not to cut through the metal strands.

2. Select two of the wires you prepared in Step 1. Attach an alligator clip to just one end of one of these wires. Clip the alligator clip to one of the electrodes on top of the electric cell. Attach another alligator clip to just one end of the second wire. Attach this alligator clip to the other electrode. Electricity enters and leaves the electric cell through the electrodes.

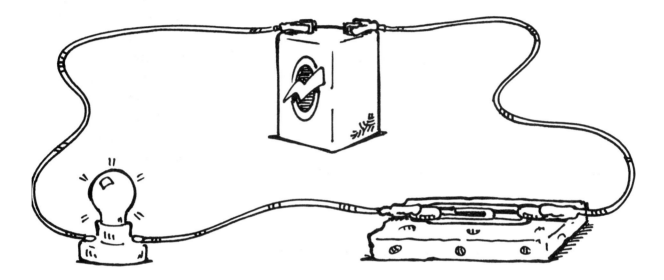

3. Select one of the two wires coming from an electrode in Step 2. Attach its free end to one of the screws on the light bulb holder. Screw the light bulb into the bulb holder.

4. Take the third wire you stripped in Step 1. Attach it to the other screw on the bulb holder. Attach an alligator clip to the free end of this wire.

5. Attach an alligator clip to the free end of the wire coming from the other electrode of the electric cell.

6. The paper clip will function as an on/off switch for your circuit. To make the switch, lay the paper clip flat on the sponge. Poke a paper fastener inside one end loop of the paper clip and push the fastener part way into the sponge. At the other end of the paper clip, push the second paper fastener partway into the sponge. This fastener should be just outside the free end of the paper clip so that the paper clip just touches it.

7. Attach the paper clip switch to the circuit. Clip one of the alligator clips from Step 5 to one of the paper fasteners on the paper clip switch. Clip the other alligator clip from Step 5 onto the other paper fastener on the switch.

8. Close the paper clip switch by swinging the free end so its tip touches the second paper fastener. What happens to the light? When you close the paper clip switch, you close the circuit so the electrons can flow. The light glows. The paper clip is a conductor because electricity flows through it. What happens when you open the paper clip switch? You break the circuit so the electrons stop flowing and the light goes out.

9. Do a conductivity test on the different objects you selected. A conductivity test shows whether an object is a conductor and carries electricity, or whether it is an insulator and does not. Unclip the entire paper clip switch and sponge from the two alligator clips and set it aside. The objects you test will replace the switch in the circuit. Select one of the objects to test. Clip the alligator clips to opposite sides of the object. If it is a conductor, electricity will flow through it to make a complete circuit, and the light will glow. If it is an insulator, electricity stops, so the light won't come on.

---

5. Do the experiment. While you do the experiment, keep notes on what you do, including things you observe and discover. Record the results of your conductivity tests on a table like the one shown below.

Test Material	Test Results (check one)	
	Conductor	Insulator
1.		
2.		
3.		
4.		
5.		
6.		
7.		

6. Write the conclusion. Summarize what happened during the experiment. Were you able to determine which of the objects you selected are insulators and which are conductors? Was your hypothesis correct? Why or why not? What would you do differently if you did the experiment again?

7. Share your findings. Create a science project display to show what you have learned from doing your experiment. Check the rules for your own school's science fair to find out the exact requirements for your display. An idea for a display is on page 7.

Background Information: Current Electricity

All objects contain tiny particles called atoms. Inside the atoms are even tinier particles called electrons. Electrons have a negative charge. In some substances, the electrons move freely about from atom to atom. These materials are called conductors. Materials in which electrons cannot move freely are called insulators.

Usually, the electrons move randomly from atom to atom in conductors. But the electrons can be made to flow in a current in just one direction. This happens when the electrons move along a pathway called a circuit. A circuit is a continuous, unbroken loop like a necklace. The movement of electrons along a circuit creates current electricity. If the circuit is broken, the electrons stop flowing in a current and start moving randomly again.

A circuit contains three parts. One part is a source of energy, such as an electric cell. ("Electric cell" is the correct term for what we usually call a battery; a true battery is actually a *grouping* of electric cells.) The second part of a circuit is a load, which is something that uses the electricity, like a light or a buzzer. The last part of a circuit is a conductor, usually a wire, through which the electrons can flow.

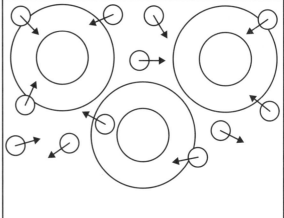

Electrons move randomly between atoms when there is no complete circuit. No current electricity is created.

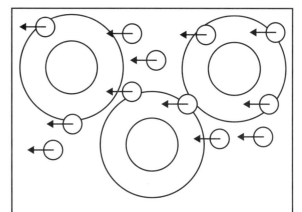

Electrons move in a current in one direction between atoms when there is a complete circuit. Current electricity is created.

Extension

With this experiment, you tested objects to see if they are conductors or insulators for electricity. Find out what kinds of objects are conductors or insulators for heat.

Category: Physical Science
Topic: Electricity and Magnetism

Project 7:
Magnets from Electricity

National Science Education Standards: Physical Science, Content Standard B: Transfer of Energy ("Energy is a property of many substances and is associated with…electricity…" and "Electrical circuits provide a means of transferring electrical energy.")

Introduction

With this project, you'll create a special type of magnet called an electromagnet.

Experiment

1. **Ask a question.** How many paper clips can an electromagnet with one nail, with four nails, with thirty coils, and with two D-cells pick up?

2. **Research the topic.** See Information Sources.

3. **Formulate a hypothesis.** How many paper clips do you think the electromagnet can pick up in each case? Write your own hypothesis.

4. **Plan the experiment.**
   A. Materials
   20-gauge insulated electrical wire (bell wire), 70 inches long total
   scissors or wire strippers
   paper clips (about 25)
   several sheets of newspaper folded in half
   two D-cells (batteries)
   electrical tape
   four 16-penny iron nails

* Information Sources

Visit your library and find books about electricity and magnets. Two suggested book are *How Science Works* by Judith Hann (New York: Reader's Digest Association, Inc., 1991) and *e.encyclopedia Science* (New York: DK Publishing, Inc. and Google, 2004). You can search the Internet by typing in this keyword: electromagnets. Also read the Background Information about magnets from electricity on page 43 of this book.

B. Procedure

1. Prepare the electrical wire for the electromagnet. To do this, cut off 60 inches (5 feet) of the wire. Use scissors or wire cutters to strip about ½ inch of the plastic insulation from both ends of the wire. Attach a paper clip to each end of the wire. To do this, loop the stripped end of the wire around one end of the paper clip. Tape one paper-clipped end of the wire to the bottom of a D-cell.

2. Set up for the experiment. Lay out the newspaper. The newspaper acts as a work surface and protects the tabletop from the batteries and wire that can get very warm during this experiment. Set the prepared wire, the D-cell, electrical tape, paper clips, and nails on the newspaper.

3. For Test #1, see how many paper clips an electromagnet with one nail will pick up. Take one of the iron nails and hold it parallel against the wire about six inches from the end taped to the D-cell. The flat end of the nail should be near the D-cell. Starting from the flat end of the nail, wrap the wire tightly around the nail for fifteen turns to create a long coil. Tape the paper clip on the loose end of the wire to the top of the D-Cell. First predict how many paper clips your electromagnet will pick up. Then hold the flat end of the nail near the paper clips. Was your prediction correct? *Caution: The D-cell, the wire, and the paper clips can get hot, so immediately detach the wire from the top of the D-cell!* While there is no current in the wire, hold the nail over the loose paper clips to see how many paper clips it picks up this time. It shouldn't pick up any because the magnetism is gone.

4. For Test #2, see how many paper clips an electromagnet with four nails will pick up. Completely unwrap the coil of wire from around the nail. Then use electrical tape to tape four nails tightly together. Wrap the wire around these nails for fifteen turns to make a long coil. Tape the paper clip on the loose end of the wire to the top of the D-cell. Predict how many paper clips the electromagnet will pick up this time. Then hold the flat ends of the nails near the paper clips. Was your prediction correct? *Immediately detach the wire from the top of the D-cell!*

5. For Test #3, see how many paper clips an electromagnet with four nails and thirty coils will pick up. Coil the wire fifteen more times around the four nails to make an even longer coil. Tape the paper clip on the loose end of the wire to the top of the D-cell. Predict how many paper clips your electromagnet will pick up. Find out by holding the flat ends of the nails over the paper clips. *Immediately detach the wire from the top of the D-cell!*

6. For Test #4, see how many paper clips an electromag-net that has two D-cells will pick up. First strip the ends off the remaining 10-inch piece of wire and at-tach paper clips to each end. Tape one paper clip end of the 10-inch piece of 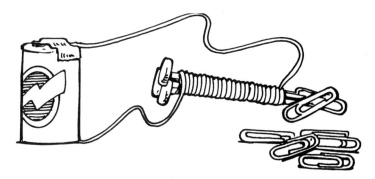 wire to the top of the D-cell you've been using. Tape the other end of that short wire to the bottom of the second D-cell. Finally, tape the paper-clipped end of the wire coming from the nails to the top of the second D-cell. How many paper clips do you predict your electromagnet will pick up now? Find out. *Immediately detach the wire from the top of the D-cell!*

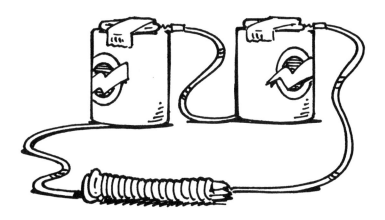

5. Do the experiment. While you do the experiment, keep notes on what you do, including things you observe and discover. Record the results of your electromagnet tests on a table like the one shown below.

Test #	Test question	Test Results
1	How many paper clips will an elecromagnet with one nail pick up?	
2	How many paper clips will an electromagnet with four nails pick up?	
3	How many paper clips will an electromagnet with thirty coils pick up?	
4	How many paper clips will an electromagnet with thirty coils and two D-cells pick up?	

6. Write the conclusion. Summarize what happened during the experiment. How did changing the number of nails, coils of wire, and D-cells affect the power of the electromagnet—and the number of paper clips it would pick up? What would you do differently if you did the experiment again?

7. Share your findings. Create a science project display to show what you have learned from doing your experiment. Check the rules for your own school's science fair to find out the exact requirements for your display. An idea for a display is on page 7.

Background Information: Magnets from Electricity

A magnet is a piece of iron or steel that attracts iron and steel. This attraction is caused by an invisible force called magnetism.

The area around a magnet is called a magnetic field. The magnetic field is strongest near the north and the south poles.

Scientists believe that iron and steel are able to become magnetic because of how their atoms behave. Millions of atoms in these metals are grouped together in domains. The domains behave like tiny magnets. When the iron or steel isn't magnetized, the domains point in random directions. When the iron and steel are magnetized, the domains line up and point in one direction. As long as the domains remain lined up, there is a magnetic force. With steel, once the domains are lined up, they tend to stay that way. The domains of iron, however, tend to quickly become random again. That's why steel magnets make permanent magnets and iron magnets are temporary magnets.

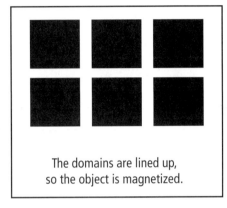
The domains are lined up, so the object is magnetized.

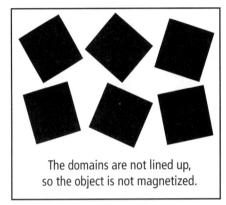
The domains are not lined up, so the object is not magnetized.

Another type of magnet called an electromagnet can be made from electricity. When an electric current flows through a wire, it creates a magnetic field around the wire. When the current stops flowing in the wire, the magnetic field disappears. The magnetic field is even stronger when the current flows through a coiled wire. If the coiled wire is also wrapped around an iron rod, the iron will become magnetized. The magnetized iron creates its own magnetic field. The coiled wire and the magnetized iron together create an electromagnet.

Extension

Find out how electromagnetism is used to power electric motors.

Category: Physical Science
Topic: Light

Project 8:
Newton's Discovery about Light

National Science Education Standards: Physical Science, Content Standard B: Transfer of Energy ("Energy is a property of many substances and is associated with…light…" and "Light interacts with matter by transmission (including refraction)…"). Science as a Human Endeavor, Content Standard G: Nature of Science: "It is part of scientific inquiry to evaluate the results of scientific investigations, experiments, observations…and the explanations proposed by other scientists;" and History of Science ("Many individuals have contributed to the traditions of science. Studying some of these individuals provides further understanding of science inquiry.")

> ****Information Sources***
>
> Visit your library and find books about light. One suggested book is *The Usborne Internet-Linked Science Encyclopedia* by Kirsteen Rogers, et al. (England: Usborne Publishing Ltd, 2002). You can search the Internet by typing in these keywords: light, diffraction, and refraction. Also read the Background Information about light on page 47 of this book.

Introduction

With this project, you can find out about Isaac Newton's discovery about light in the year 1666.

Experiment

1. **Ask a question.** What did Isaac Newton find when he used diffraction and refraction to bend light waves in 1666?

2. **Research the topic.** See Information Sources

3. **Formulate a hypothesis.** What do you think? Write your own hypothesis.

4. **Plan the experiment.**
   A. **Materials**
      flashlight with strong light
      lightweight cardboard (cardboard from a cereal box works well)
      pencil
      scissors
      ruler
      sharp knife
      tape
      one *clear* liter-sized soda bottle
      tap water
      clipboard
      sheets of white paper
      colored pencils

B. Procedure

1. Make a diffraction shield to bend the light waves coming from the flashlight. To do this, stand the flashlight face down on the cardboard. Trace a circle around the part of the lens that touches the cardboard. Cut out the circle. Have an adult use the sharp knife and ruler to cut a slit an eighth of an inch wide in the center of the cardboard. Center the cardboard on the lens of the flashlight, being sure you can see the light bulb through the slit. Tape the cardboard to the flashlight. In Newton's experiment, the sunlight was diffracted through a hole in his window shutters. In your experiment, the light from the flashlight will be diffracted through the diffraction shield.

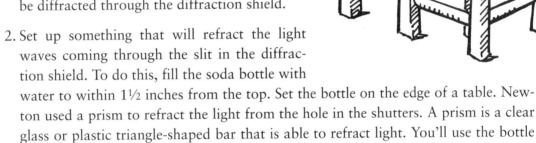

2. Set up something that will refract the light waves coming through the slit in the diffraction shield. To do this, fill the soda bottle with water to within 1½ inches from the top. Set the bottle on the edge of a table. Newton used a prism to refract the light from the hole in the shutters. A prism is a clear glass or plastic triangle-shaped bar that is able to refract light. You'll use the bottle of water in place of a prism.

3. Set up the rest of the experiment. Set a chair in front of the soda bottle. On the seat of the chair, place a clipboard with a sheet of white paper attached to it.

4. Do the experiment. You will need someone to help you. Turn out the lights—this experiment works best in a very dark room. Stand beside the chair and wait for the water in the soda bottle to be still. Shine the flashlight at an angle into the soda bottle so that the beam reaches the white paper on the chair. The slit in the diffraction shield on the flashlight should be vertical. Move the flashlight around until you see something other than white light shining on the white paper on the clipboard. Do you see what Newton saw during his own experiment? If you do, ask your helper to hold the flashlight still in that same position. Use the colored pencils to quickly trace what you see on the white paper. When you are done, write the time on the sketch and save it. Repeat the experiment several more times. You can also try holding the diffraction shield on the flashlight in a horizontal position.

5. **Do the experiment.** While you do the experiment, keep notes on what you do, including things you observe and discover. Save the sheets you sketched during the experiment.

6. **Write the conclusion.** Summarize what happened during the experiment. What appeared on the white paper? What do you think caused it to appear? You might do some research on the visible spectrum to find out. Study the sketches you made with the colored pencils. Is there a similar pattern on each of the sketches? What would you do differently if you did the experiment again?

7. **Share your findings.** Create a science project display to show what you have learned from doing your experiment. Check the rules for your own school's science fair to find out the exact requirements for your display. An idea for a display is on page 7.

Background Information: Light

In 1666, a scientist named Isaac Newton was experimenting with light. Light is a form of energy we can see. Like other forms of energy, light moves in waves. It also usually moves in straight lines. But Newton was able to bend the light waves. When he did, he saw something amazing. How did he bend the light waves? And what did he discover?

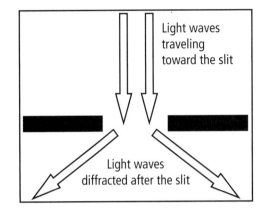

Light waves traveling toward the slit

Light waves diffracted after the slit

Newton bent the light waves using both diffraction and refraction. Diffraction happens when light waves pass through a slit. The small space causes the waves to spread out and bend or diffract. The thinner the slit, the more the waves spread out and diffract.

Refraction is another way that light waves bend. Refraction happens when light waves bend or refract as they travel between substances with different densities. Denser substances have more mass in a certain volume than less dense substances. Light waves move slower and refract more through a denser substance than through a less dense one. In order for the light waves to refract, they must meet the new substance at an angle. If you put a drinking straw in a glass of water at an angle, the straw will appear to bend. That's because the light waves from the straw travel slower and refract more in the denser water than in the less dense air.

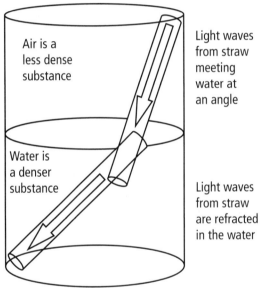

Air is a less dense substance

Water is a denser substance

Light waves from straw meeting water at an angle

Light waves from straw are refracted in the water

So what did Isaac Newton discover when he used diffraction and refraction to bend light waves? You can do this experiment to find out.

Extension

Find out more about Isaac Newton and his many accomplishments.

Category: Physical Science
Topic: Sound

Project 9:
How's That Sound?

National Science Education Standards: Physical Science, Content Standard B: Transfer of Energy ("Energy is a property of many substances and is associated with...sound. Energy is transferred in many ways.")

Introduction

With this project, you'll find out if sound travels better through a gas, a liquid, or a solid.

Experiment

1. **Ask a question.** Does sound travel best through a gas, a liquid, or a solid?

2. **Research the topic.** See Information Sources.

3. **Formulate a hypothesis.** What do you think? Write your own hypothesis.

4. **Plan the experiment.**
   A. Materials
   two 1-gallon heavy-duty zipper lock plastic bags
   water
   hardback book about 9" wide by 10" long by 1½" inches thick
   wind-up clock or plastic kitchen timer that ticks loudly
   plastic bowl that the clock or timer will fit inside
   radio or television inside a bedroom or other room that has a door

> *** Information Sources**
>
> Visit your library and find books about sound. One suggested book is *How Science Works* by Judith Hann (New York: Reader's Digest Association, Inc., 1991). You can search the Internet by typing in these keywords: sound and sound waves. Also read the Background Information about sound on page 51 of this book.

B. Procedure

1. Seal the zipper locks partway on the two plastic bags so there is about a 1-inch opening. Hold one of the bags in a sink and fill it with water through the opening. Seal the zipper all the way. Hold the other bag to your mouth and blow through the opening to fill it with air like a balloon. Seal the zipper all the way. *Caution: Be careful that you don't cover your nose with the plastic bag while you blow it up.*

2. Place the clock or timer at one end of a long table. Make sure the clock or timer is ticking. Turn the plastic bowl upside down and cover the clock or timer.

3. Set the bag of air flat on the table. Next to it, place the bag of water so it is also flat. Then set the book next to the water. The water will be the liquid for the experiment, and the air will be the gas. The book will be the solid.

4. For Test #1, you'll listen to the ticking clock through each of the three items—the bag of air, the bag of water, and the book. Predict through which of the three items you'll be able to hear the ticking of the clock the loudest. Which will be the softest? Then test your prediction. Sit in a chair in front of the items. Lean over and place one of your ears firmly against the bag of air. Plug the other ear with your finger. Can you hear the ticking from the clock or timer? Is it loud, medium, or soft? Repeat with the bag of water, then the book. Through which of the three objects could you hear the ticking the loudest? Which was the softest?

5. For Test #2, you'll hold the three items against a door and listen to a radio or television in the other room. Before doing the test, check to see if the bag of air needs to be blown up again, and check to make sure the bag of water isn't leaking. Turn on the radio or television and adjust the sound to a soft level. Leave the room and close the door behind you. Predict through which of the three items you'll hear the sound the best. Then stand against the door outside the room, hold the bag of air, and press it against your ear. Plug your other ear and see if you can hear the radio or television sound through the bag of air. Repeat with the bag of water and then the book. Was your prediction correct?

SOLID   LIQUID   GAS

5. Do the experiment. While you do the experiment, keep notes on what you do, including things you observe and discover. Record the results of your sound tests on a table like the one shown below.

Object	Test #1 Listening to ticking timer or clock on a table (check one)			Test #2 Listening to radio or TV through a wall (check one)		
	Loudest	Medium	Softest	Loudest	Medium	Softest
Gas: Bag of air						
Liquid: Bag of water						
Solid: Book						

6. Write the conclusion. Summarize what happened during the experiment. Could you hear the sounds loudest through the bag of air, the bag of water, or the book? Which was the second loudest? Which was the softest? What would you do differently if you did the experiment again?

7. Share your findings. Create a science project display to show what you have learned from doing your experiment. Check the rules for your own school's science fair to find out the exact requirements for your display. An idea for a display is on page 7.

Background Information: Sound

Sound is a form of energy we can hear. Like other forms of energy, sound is carried by waves. The type of wave that carries sound is called a longitudinal wave. A longitudinal wave is made up of vibrating particles that move back and forth in the direction that the wave moves.

When you bang a drum, the skin on the drum starts to vibrate. When the skin vibrates outward it pushes out on the air molecules surrounding it, squeezing them together. When the skin vibrates inward, it leaves space for the air molecules to stretch back out. As the skin continues vibrating, it creates a series of waves that move out through the air in all directions. These waves are called sound waves.

Sound waves are invisible. People cannot see them passing through the air. But people can hear them when they reach their ears. That's because the sound waves vibrate their ear drums.

Sound waves, like all longitudinal waves, depend upon matter to move them. That's why sound waves not only move through air, but they also move through liquids and solids. The more matter the substance contains, the better the sound waves move through it. Sound waves cannot move through a vacuum because a vacuum contains no matter.

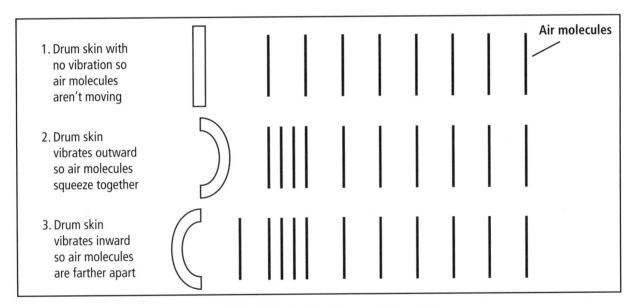

SOUND WAVES FROM A DRUM SKIN

Extension

Make a cup-and-string phone. Punch a small hole in the bottoms of two empty yogurt cups or tin cans. Push the ends of a long piece of string through the bottoms of each cup. Tie paper clips to the ends of the strings inside the cups. Have a partner take one cup and you take the other. Move away from each other until the string is tight. To talk, hold the rim of the cup around your mouth and speak clearly. To listen, hold the rim of the cup to your ear. How does the cup-and-string phone transmit sound waves?

Category: Life Science
Topic: Flower reproduction

Project 10:
Flowers from Flowers

National Science Education Standards: Life Science, Content Standard C: Reproduction and Heredity ("Reproduction is a characteristic of all living systems" and "Plants…reproduce sexually—the egg and sperm are produced in the flowers of flowering plants. An egg and sperm unite to begin development of a new individual. That new individual receives genetic information from its mother (via the egg) and its father (via the sperm). Sexually produced offspring are never identical to either of their parents.")

Introduction

With this project, you'll examine different kinds of flowers to see what their reproductive structures look like and how they are pollinated.

Experiment

1. **Ask a question.** What kinds of reproductive structures do different kinds of flowers have and how are the flowers pollinated?

2. **Research the topic.** See Information Sources.

3. **Formulate a hypothesis.** What do you think? Write your own hypothesis.

4. **Plan the experiment.**
   A. Materials

   two to three different samples of flowers, such as poppies, tulips, daffodils, pansies, buttercups, and hibiscus
   scissors or plant pruning shears
   a jar of water for each flower sample
   heavy paper plates or Styrofoam plates
   hand lens (magnifying glass)
   sharp knife

   tweezers
   pencil
   colored pencils
   sheets of white sketching paper
   paper clips
   optional: flower buds for each flower sample

> **** Information Sources***
>
> Visit your library and find books about plants and flowers. Two suggested books are *How Nature Works* by David Burnie (New York: The Reader's Digest Association, Inc., 1991) and *Eyewitness Books: Plant* by David Burnie (New York: DK Publishing, Inc., 2004). You can search the Internet by typing in these keywords: flowers and flower reproduction. Check out "How Flowering Plants Reproduce" on the Zephyrus Web site at www.zephyrus.co.uk/flowerrepro. Also read the Background Information about flower reproduction on pages 55–56 of this book.

B. Procedure

1. Collect the flower samples. Use the scissors or plant pruning shears to cut the flowers from the stems. Try to cut them so you have at least six inches of the stem. Store the flower samples in jars of water until you are ready to study them. *Caution: Be sure to first get permission from the owner of a flower before cutting it. Do not take flowers, including wild flowers, growing in parks or other public areas.*

2. Examine one of your flower samples. Take the flower out of the water and lay it on a paper plate. Examine it with a hand lens. On one sheet of sketching paper, draw the flower. Somewhere on the front of this sheet of paper, write "Sample 1: Whole Flower." Also write the date you found the flower and its location. It is not important to know the name of the flower for this project, but if you do know it, write the name on the sheet of paper.

3. Take the flower apart and examine its parts. Remove the sepals and count them. Then remove the petals and count them. Now try to find as many of the male and female reproductive structures as possible. Use the knife, scissors, and tweezers as needed. Gently remove the reproductive structures from the flower, one at a time. Examine them and count them. If you find the ovary, cut it in half and look inside it. Set all the flower parts out on the plate in the approximate order they appeared in the flower. When you are done, draw the reproductive structures on a clean sheet of paper. If you know the name of any of the reproductive structures (sometimes it is difficult to tell on some flowers), label those structures on your drawing. On the sheet of paper, write "Sample 1: Flower Reproductive Structures." Clip this drawing together with the drawing from step 2.

4. From what you have observed of the flower sample, how do you think it is pollinated? Examine the pollen grains, and the shape, color, and scent of the flower. Also think of how the flower grew on the plant and if you saw any insects or other animals working on the flower.

5. Repeat steps 2 and 4 for the other flower samples you found. On the sketches, label the second flower "Sample 2," and the third "Sample 3."

6. Optional: If you have samples of the flower buds, examine them. Take them apart and count the pieces. Set the pieces on a clean paper plate. How do the buds compare to the whole flower? You can sketch the bud parts on a fresh sheet of paper and clip it with the other drawings for the same flower.

5. **Do the experiment.** While you do the experiment, keep notes on what you do, including things you observe and discover. Record information about the flowers and their reproductive structures on a table like the one shown below. Store the table with your sketches of the flowers.

Test #	Date found	Kind of flower (if known)	Sepals (write in how many of each)	Petals (write in how many of each)	Reproductive structures found (write in how many of each)					How I think the flower is pollinated (check one)		
					Stamen (male)		**Carpel** (female)					
					Anther	Filament	Stigma	Style	Ovary	Animals	Wind	Other
1												
2												
3												

6. **Write the conclusion.** Summarize what happened during the experiment. What reproductive structures did you find in the different flower samples? How do you think each of your sample flowers is pollinated? What makes you think that? What would you do differently if you did the experiment again?

7. **Share your findings.** Create a science project display to show what you have learned from doing your experiment. Check the rules for your own school's science fair to find out the exact requirements for your display. An idea for a display is on page 7.

Background Information: Flower Reproduction

To help assure that plants and animals continue to live on throughout the ages, they go through a process called reproduction. Reproduction means a plant or animal produces a new organism like itself.

Plants called angiosperms reproduce through their flowers. The type of reproduction that takes place in the flowers is called sexual reproduction. In order for sexual reproduction to take place, flowers contain both male and female reproductive organs. For many angiosperms, both male and female organs are found on the same plant.

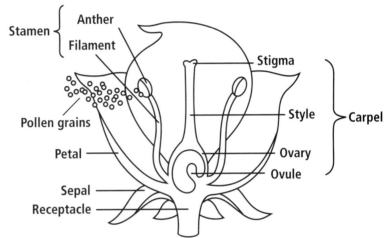

The male organ of a flower is the stamen. It is made up of a sac-like anther that's held up by a long stalk called a filament. The anther produces grains of pollen, which are the male sex cells.

The female organ is the carpel (or pistil). The stigma at the top of the carpel is sticky so it attracts pollen. The stigma is supported on a stalk called a style. At the base of the style is the ovary, which holds the female sex cells. The female sex cells are tiny eggs called ovules.

In order for sexual reproduction to happen in the flowers, the pollen and ovules must join together. This process is called pollination. Usually the pollen comes from one plant, and the ovules come from another plant of the same kind.

There are several ways that the pollen of one flower can reach the other flower. In some angiosperms, the pollen is carried by the wind. These plants usually produce a lot of pollen, and each grain of pollen is light enough to float through the air. The flower structures of these plants are also often exposed, making it easier for the wind to reach them.

For many angiosperms, the pollen is carried by insects and animals such as bees, butterflies, birds, and bats. These plants often contain brightly-colored flowers to attract the animals. The flowers also usually have a scent and produce a sweet liquid called nectar, which the insects and animals like.

When the pollen reaches the other flower, it sticks to the stigma. From the stigma, a tube forms down through the style to the ovary. Male cells from the pollen travel down the tube and join with the ovule. This process is called fertilization.

After fertilization, the ovary develops into a fruit that contains the seeds. The flower petals are no longer needed, so they drop off.

After the seeds fall to the ground, new plants grow from them. The new plants have tight flower buds. The buds have protective covers called sepals that enclose unopened petals. Once the pollen inside the bud is ready for pollination, the sepals fold back. Then the buds open out to reveal flowers that are prepared to reproduce.

With sexual reproduction, the new plants are the same kind of plant as the original plants that supplied the pollen and the ovule. But the new plant is not identical to the original plants. For example, Oriental poppy plants always create new Oriental poppy plants. But the flowers on one of the new plants might be a different color from the flowers on the original plants.

Extension

In this project you studied how a plant reproduces sexually. Plants can also reproduce asexually. Find out about asexual reproduction of plants and the different ways it can be done.

Category: Life Science
Topic: Evolution

Project 11:
Adaptations of Wild Birds

National Science Education Standards: Life Science, Content Standard C: Regulation and Behavior ("An organism's behavior evolves through adaptation to its environment. How a species moves, obtains food, reproduces, and responds to danger are based in the species' evolutionary history.") and Diversity and Adaptations of Organisms ("Biological evolution accounts for the diversity of species developed through gradual processes over many generations. Species acquire many of their unique characteristics through biological adaptation, which involves the selection of naturally occurring variations in populations. Biological adaptations include changes in structures, behaviors, or physiology that enhance survival and reproductive success in a particular environment.")

Introduction

With this project, you'll study several different kinds of birds in your area to see what adaptations they have and why those adaptations are beneficial to the bird.

Experiment

1. **Ask a question.** What kinds of adaptations do different birds have, and how do they help the bird survive?

2. **Research the topic.** See Information Sources.

3. **Formulate a hypothesis.** What do you think? Write your own hypothesis.

4. **Plan the experiment.**
   A. Materials
   a notebook (fill a small three-ring binder with sheets of binder paper and sheets of plain white paper)
   pencil
   colored pencils
   optional: binoculars and bird identification book

> **** Information Sources***
> Visit your library and find books about evolution and about birds. Two suggested books are *Eyewitness Birds* by David Burnie (New York: DK Publishing, Inc., 2004) and *e.encyclopedia Science* (New York: DK Publishing, Inc. and Google, 2004). You can search the Internet by typing in these keywords: evolution and birds. Also read the Background Information about evolution and adaptations on page 59 of this book.

B. Procedure

1. Carefully observe three different wild birds at your school or in your neighborhood. As you study each bird, ask yourself the following questions. What does its beak, body, and feet look like? What is the color and shape of its feathers? What sounds does it make? What does it eat? What unusual features does it have? Does it move by flying, swimming, and/or walking? Does it have babies, and can you see a nest? What is its habitat (the place where it lives) like? Try to observe the same bird on several different days to see if you discover anything new. As you observe each bird, write detailed notes about it on sheets of binder paper in your notebook. Sketch a picture of the bird on a sheet of plain white paper in your notebook and color it in. Optional: Use binoculars to help you observe a bird that is far away. Also try looking up the bird in a bird identification book to find more information you can add to your notebook. Be sure to write this information in your own words.

2. When you are done studying each bird, look back through the notes and sketches in your notebook. For each bird, think about what beneficial traits or adaptations it has. How do you think the adaptations help the bird survive today in its habitat? For example, if the bird has a thick bill, it might help the bird crack the nuts that it eats. If the bird has feathers that are dull and speckled, the feathers might help it hide in the bushes from larger birds or other predators. If it has webbed feet and lives near water, it can swim easily. Write your ideas in your notebook.

5. **Do the experiment.** While you do the experiment, be sure to take notes and make sketches in your notebook.

6. **Write the conclusion.** Summarize what happened during the experiment. What were the adaptations for the birds you studied? What would you do differently if you did the experiment again?

7. **Share your findings.** Create a science project display to show what you have learned from doing your experiment. Check the rules for your own school's science fair to find out the exact requirements for your display. An idea for a display is on page 7.

Background Information: Evolution and Adaptations

Evolution is the gradual development of organisms from earlier forms of life. An organism is any living thing, including plants and animals.

Through evolution, the first tiny organisms that appeared on earth billions of years ago slowly changed or evolved into the huge variety of animals like fish and horses—and even humans—that we know today. Evolution still continues, meaning creatures of the future may look far different from the ones we know today.

In the middle 1800s, a scientist named Charles Darwin was the first to provide a believable theory about how plants and animals can change over time. He called his theory *natural selection* because nature determines which animals survive and which do not.

Darwin's theory says that animals produce a lot of babies or offspring, but not all of them survive. Only the fittest animals do. The fittest animals are the ones which have traits that help them survive in their particular environment. Traits are characteristics, like fur color, that the animal inherits from its parents. The traits that a particular kind of animal inherits can vary. For example, for an imaginary bear we'll call the X-Bear, some offspring might be born with dark brown fur, while others might be born with bright yellow fur.

Those traits that help an animal survive are called adaptations. If the imaginary X-Bears in the example above live in a dark mountain forest and must sneak up on their prey, which color of bear is most likely to survive? The bear with the dark brown fur. Dark fur is an adaptation for X-Bears. The X-Bears with bright yellow fur have a hard time capturing their prey without being seen, so they often starve. In this case, yellow fur is not an adaptation.

Animals that survive because they have adaptations usually have healthy offspring. These offspring can inherit the adaptations. As the adaptations are passed on from generation to generation, many of the animals end up with the adaptations. In the X-Bear example, the bears with the dark brown fur adaptation continue to reproduce until there are many of them with the dark fur. The bears with yellow fur decrease in number until they could eventually die off. The fittest animals survive, while the unfit ones often do not.

Darwin came up with his theory of natural selection by studying a variety of plants and animals around the world. One kind of animal he studied were finches living on the Galapagos Islands in the Pacific Ocean. He discovered many different kinds of finches, each living on a different island. Some finches had thick beaks for cracking the nuts and seeds. Other finches had long beaks for reaching into trees for insects. Darwin concluded that at one time, there was just one kind of finch. Over time, the finch developed the particular kinds of adaptations that helped it survive in the various environments of the different islands.

Category: Earth and Space Science
Topic: Water Cycle

Project 12:
Water Cycle in a Bottle

National Science Education Standards: Earth and Space Science, Content Standard D: Structure of the Earth System ("Water, which covers the majority of the earth's surface, circulates through the crust, ocean, and atmosphere in what is known as the water cycle.") and Earth in the Solar System ("The sun is the major source of energy for phenomena on the earth's surface, such as growth of plants…and the water cycle.")

Introduction

With this project, you'll create a miniature version of the water cycle and see how it benefits plants.

Experiment

1. **Ask a question.** Do plants grow better with the water cycle or without?

2. **Research the topic.** See Information Sources.

3. **Formulate a hypothesis.** The water cycle helps plants grow better because it provides a regular supply of moisture.

4. **Plan the experiment.**
   A. Materials
   — two 10-ounce (296 ml) *clear* plastic disposable drinking cups
   — potting soil
   measuring cup
   water
   spoon
   two small, identical house plants (philodendron or spider plants work well)
   — liter size soda bottle with lid (thoroughly rinse bottle and remove label)
   tape
   several sheets of facial tissue or bathroom tissue
   pencil

> * **Information Sources**
> Visit your library and find books about the water cycle. One suggested book is *My Water Comes from the Mountains* by Tiffany Fourment (Maryland: Roberts Rinehart Publishers, 2004). You can search the Internet by typing in this keyword: water cycle. Also read the Background Information about the water cycle on page 63 of this book.

B. Procedure

1. Fill the two cups with potting soil. Add ⅓ cup of water to the soil in each cup (add ½ cup of water if the weather is hot). Gently push the small spoon up and down through the soil to mix the water in.

2. Use the small spoon to dig a hole in the soil at the edge of one cup. Put a plant in the hole. Push the plant against the side of the cup so you can see the plant's lower stem and roots. Smooth the soil around the plant. Repeat for the other cup.

3. Create a water cycle chamber for just one of the plants. To do this, have an adult cut the bottom of the soda bottle off about 2 inches from the bottom. Set one of the plant cups in the bottom of the bottle. Leave the plant inside, and tape the top of the bottle to the bottom. Use just a few pieces of tape so you can later check the plant. Screw the cap on the bottle. What steps of the water cycle will occur in the water cycle chamber? All the steps. Evaporation occurs when heat from the room or the sun warms the water in the soil and turns it to water vapor. Condensation occurs when the water vapor condenses on the plastic inside the top of the water cycle chamber and turns to water droplets. Precipitation occurs when the water droplets join together and become heavy enough to fall back on the soil. Also, through transpiration, the plant absorbs water and returns it to the air in the chamber. For the uncovered plant, there is only evaporation from the soil and transpiration from the plant.

4. Set the water cycle chamber and the uncovered plant side-by-side near a window where they get bright light, but not direct sun. Predict which of the plants will be the healthiest in a week.

5. In a week, study the plants. Do they look healthy? Remove a pinch of soil from each cup and set it on a sheet of facial tissue. Which soil sample has the most moisture? Are there drops of water in the top of the water cycle chamber? Set the plants back near the window. Do not add water to either cup.

6. Continue studying the plants once a week for the next three weeks. But do not add water to either cup.

5. Do the experiment. While you do the experiment, keep notes on what you do, including things you observe and discover. Each week when you study the plants, soil, and water cycle chamber, record the results on a table like the one shown below.

Week # _____	Condition and health of plants and roots (describe)	Amount of moisture in soil (check one)			Are there drops of water at the top of the water cycle chamber? (check one)	
		Wet	Damp	Dry	Yes	No
Plant in water cycle chamber						
Uncovered plant not in water cycle chamber						

6. Write the conclusion. Summarize what happened during the experiment. Which plant was the healthiest at the end of the experiment: the plant in the water cycle chamber, or the uncovered plant? Why? What do you think would happen to life on Earth if there was no water cycle? What would you do differently if you did the experiment again?

7. Share your findings. Create a science project display to show what you have learned from doing your experiment. Check the rules for your own school's science fair to find out the exact requirements for your display. An idea for a display is on page 7.

which plant heathiest?
WHY?

What would happen if we didn't have water cycle?
What would you do different if you did this again.

Background Information: The Water Cycle

The water cycle is the constant movement of water on Earth between the ground and the sky. The three main steps of the water cycle are evaporation, condensation, and precipitation.

During evaporation, heat from the sun warms water on the surface of Earth. The heat causes water molecules to speed up in the water. Eventually, some molecules escape into the air as water vapor. This process where liquid water turns into water vapor is called evaporation.

The next step is condensation. The water vapor continues rising up higher in the atmosphere, where the air grows colder and colder. Molecules in cold air are closer together than in warm air. This means cold air can't hold as much water vapor as hot air does. Eventually, the air becomes too cold to hold any more water vapor. When that happens,

the water vapor turns back into visible water droplets that form around dust in the air. This is condensation. When many of the water droplets cluster together, they form clouds.

The last step is precipitation. The tiny water droplets that make up a cloud join together to make larger drops. If they become too heavy for the air to hold, the water drops fall to the ground as precipitation. Depending on the temperature of the air, the precipitation can be rain, snow, sleet, or hail.

Most of the precipitation ends up back in the ocean, which covers three-quarters of our planet. Once the water is back on Earth, it eventually evaporates, continuing the water cycle.

Plants are also part of the water cycle. They absorb water from the soil into their roots and release it back into the air as water vapor. This process is called transpiration.

Extension

Whenever you turn on a faucet, water automatically streams out. But did you ever wonder where that water comes from? Find out what the source of water is in your town, where it is stored, and what route it takes to get to your school or home.

Category: Earth and Space Science
Topic: Weather/Clouds

Project 13:
Cloud Charts

National Science Education Standards: Earth and Space Science,
Content Standard D: Structure of the Earth System ("Clouds affect weather and
climate.")

Introduction

With this project, you'll create a cloud chart showing ten different types of clouds.

Experiment

1. **Ask a question.** Can clouds help forecast the weather?

2. **Research the topic.** See Information Sources.

3. **Formulate a hypothesis.** Clouds can help forecast the weather because different kinds of clouds are associated with different kinds of weather.

4. **Plan the experiment.**
   A. Materials
   5 sheets of 9" x 12" construction paper
   scissors
   clear tape
   hole punch
   cotton balls
   several pieces of white facial tissue
   glue
   pencil
   yarn cut into eighteen 6" strips
   scissors

*** Information Sources**

Visit your library and find books about clouds. Two suggested books are *Measuring Weather: Cloud Cover* by Alan Rodgers and Angella Streluk (Illinois: Heinemann Library, 2003) and *National Audubon Society First Field Guide: Weather* by Jonathan D. Kahl (New York: Scholastic, Inc., 1998). You can search the Internet by typing in these keywords: clouds and weather. You can also search The Weather Channel Web site at www.weatherchannel.com. Also read the Background Information about clouds on page 68 of this book.

B. Procedure

1. Prepare the cloud chart. To do this, cut the sheets of construction paper in half widthwise. Each half sheet of paper will be a page of the cloud chart that shows a different type of cloud. Mark two holes about 5 inches apart along the longer top and bottom edges of each page. Put a short piece of tape on each marking on one side of the paper to reinforce it. Punch holes through the paper and tape at each marking.

2. Form pieces of cotton into the ten different cloud shapes. To make wispy clouds, tear off small pieces of cotton and slowly stretch them out. To make rolls of clouds, roll a small piece of cotton in your hands. To make sheet or veil-like clouds, pull apart the two layers of a sheet of facial tissue so you have a single, thin layer, then cut out a rectangle shape for the cloud. Before making the cirrostratus cloud, draw a yellow ring around the edge of a small circle of white paper to make the sun's halo, and glue the circle to the center of the construction paper page from Step 1. Before making the altostratus cloud, draw a solid yellow sun on a small circle of paper and glue to the middle of the construction paper page. To darken a cloud, rub a pencil lead back and forth across a sheet of scrap paper, and then rub the cotton or tissue over the lead on the paper. Look at the cloud table on the following page to help you make the clouds.

3. Attach the clouds to the construction paper pages of the cloud chart. To do this, lay one of the pages on a table so one of its longer, hole-punched sides faces you. The tape-reinforced side of the page should be facing down against the table. Glue the cotton cloud to the page. Tape the facial tissue clouds. For the cumulonimbus cloud, leave space at the top of the page and draw several arrows pointing upward to show that the top of the cloud can be very high. Leave about two inches of space on the page below each of the clouds. In this space, write the name of the cloud, its height, and both the current weather and the forecasted weather that's usually associated with the type of cloud. If you wish, you can instead write or type this information on white slips of paper and glue them onto the page. Lay out the cloud sheets when you are done so they can dry thoroughly.

4. Lay out the ten cloud pages on the floor in one long vertical column, with the hole-punched sides facing each other. The clouds should be in order from the highest cloud in the sky (cirrus) to the lowest (cumulonimbus). Tie two short strips of yarn between the holes at the bottom of one page and the holes at the top of the page just below it. Make the ties loose so you can fold up the pages later. When you are done tying the pages together, you will have one long cloud chart.

5. Attach your cloud chart to a wall. When you are done with the chart, you can fold it up accordion-style and store it like a book.

6. For the next two weeks, observe the sky each day at the same time of day. Record the date, and the types of clouds you observe. Use your cloud chart to help you. You might see several different types of clouds, or you might see no clouds. If you're not sure of a type of cloud try to determine if it is one of the three main types (cirrus, stratus, or cumulus) and call it by that name. Also record what the weather is when you observe the clouds. Is it sunny or cloudy? Warm or cold? Calm or windy? Dry or stormy?

5. Do the experiment. While you observe the sky, keep notes on the types of clouds and the weather you see. Record the results on a table like the one shown below.

	Date:	Date:	Date:	Date:	Date:
	Weather:	Weather:	Weather:	Weather:	Weather:
	Clouds observed (check one)	**Clouds observed** (check one)	**Clouds observed** (check one)	**Clouds observed** (check one)	**Clouds observed** (check one)
1. Cirrus					
2. Cirrocumulus					
3. Cirrostratus					
4. Altocumulus					
5. Altostratus					
6. Stratocumulus					
7. Stratus					
8. Nimbostratus					
9. Cumulus					
10. Cumulonimbus					
No clouds					

6. Write the conclusion. Summarize what happened during the experiment. What did you learn about the clouds? Did the clouds you saw on one day help forecast the weather that you saw on the following day? What would you do differently if you did the experiment again?

7. Share your findings. Create a science project display to show what you have learned from doing your experiment. Check the rules for your own school's science fair to find out the exact requirements for your display. An idea for a display is on page 7.

Background Information: Clouds

Clouds are masses of water droplets or ice crystals floating in the air. They form when an invisible gas called water vapor rises in the sky. Air becomes colder and colder the farther above Earth it is. The colder the air is, the less water vapor it can hold. Eventually, the water vapor rises to a height where the air cannot hold any more water vapor. When this happens, the water vapor condenses. This means it clings to dust or smoke particles in the air and becomes visible as water droplets. The water droplets are so tiny that they float in the air. If many droplets mass together, they form a cloud. If the cloud condenses high in the atmosphere where it is extremely cold, the cloud is made up of ice crystals instead of water droplets.

There are three basic types of clouds. Stratus clouds are broad sheets or layers that form when large areas of moist air rise slowly and condense. Cumulus clouds are lumpy puffs that form when pockets of warm air rise. Cirrus clouds are thin, wispy clouds that form when moist air rises high into the atmosphere and condenses into ice crystals, which are blown about by winds. Clouds appear in so many different shapes that the three types are further classified into ten different types. The ten are primarily combinations of the three basic cloud types. Note: Nimbus refers to rain, and alto refers to medium-level clouds.

Certain types of weather are associated with each cloud type. Clouds can also help forecast the weather.

Extension

Collect magazine pictures or take photographs of the different types of clouds. Glue each picture or photo on the back of its corresponding cotton cloud page.

Cloud type	Description	Height	Current weather	Forecast weather	
1. Cirrus	Thin and wispy strands; made of ice crystals	over 16,500' (5,000 m)	fair, if sky is clear	stormy if sky covered	1
2. Cirrocumulus	Many very small, all-white puffs arranged in waves or ripples; made of ice crystals; least common cloud	over 16,500' (5,000 m)	fair	rain likely	2
3. Cirrostratus	Thin, veil-like layer of clouds, creating glowing halo around the sun; made of ice crystals	over 16,500' (5,000 m)	lightly overcast	precipitation possible	3
4. Altocumulus	Many medium-sized white and gray cotton ball clouds with shadows; in mountains, clouds may look like a flying saucer; made of water droplets	6,500' to 16,500' (2,000 m to 5,000 m)	fair	precipitation possible	4
5. Altostatus	Blue-gray sheet-like layer covering much or all of the sky; sometimes called a "watery sky"; makes the sun look hazy; often appears with altocumulus; made of water droplets	6,500' to 16,500' (2,000 m to 5,000 m)	lightly overcast; possible precipitation	precipitation likely over a wide area	5
6. Stratocumulus	Many large, dark puffs or rolls arranged in rows or waves; flat base and jagged top; common cloud; made of water droplets	2,000' to 6,500' (600 m to 2,000 m)	fair, but light precipitation if clouds thick	fair, or light drizzle	6
7. Stratus	Gray, widely-spread sheet; made of water droplets	up to 6,500' (2,000 m)	overcast; drizzle	drizzle or light rain	7
8. Nimbostratus	Thick, dark-gray, widely spread sheet; made of water droplets	up to 6,500' (2,000 m)	overcast; wide rain	continuous precipitation	8
9. Cumulus	Lumpy puffs, usually with flat bottoms; made of water droplets	up to 20,000' (6,000 m)	fair if clouds scattered	fair	9
10. Cumulonimbus	Tall, lumpy puffs extending high into the sky; sometimes has a flat top that points out to the side like an anvil; made mostly of water droplets, but top can be ice crystals	up to 60,000' (18,000 m)	stormy; lightning and thunder; strong winds; possible tornadoes	colder weather in winter	10

Category: Earth and Space Science
Topic: The Seasons

Project 14:
Seasons around the Sun

National Science Education Standards: Earth and Space Science, Content Standard D: Earth in the Solar System ("Seasons result from variations in the amount of the sun's energy hitting the surface due to the tilt of the earth's rotation on its axis and the length of the day.")

Introduction

With this project, you'll make a model of the sun and Earth's orbit around it to find out about the seasons.

Activity

1. **Ask a question.** Why is it warmer in the summer than in the winter in the Northern Hemisphere?

2. **Research the topic.** See Information Sources.

3. **Formulate a hypothesis.** What do you think? Write your own hypothesis.

4. **Plan the experiment.**
   A. Materials

three 10-ounce (296 ml) clear plastic disposable drinking cups	pencil
small flashlight (about 6" long)	ruler
masking tape	push pin
one 5" diameter Styrofoam ball	rubber band
bread knife (for adult use)	laundry marker
one 2½" diameter Styrofoam ball	masking tape
glue	one photocopy of the "Seasons around the Sun" pattern (on the following page), enlarged and printed on 11" x 17" paper
scissors	
paint	
brushes	crayons (optional)

* *Information Sources*

Visit your library and find books about the seasons. One suggested book is *The Kingfisher Young People's Book of the Universe* (New York: Kingfisher, 2001). You can search the Internet by typing in this keyword: seasons. If you want to see how sunlight hits on different parts of the Earth throughout the different seasons of the year, visit www.ameritech.net/users/paulcarlisle/earthviewer. Also read the Background Information about the seasons on page 74 of this book.

Name: _____

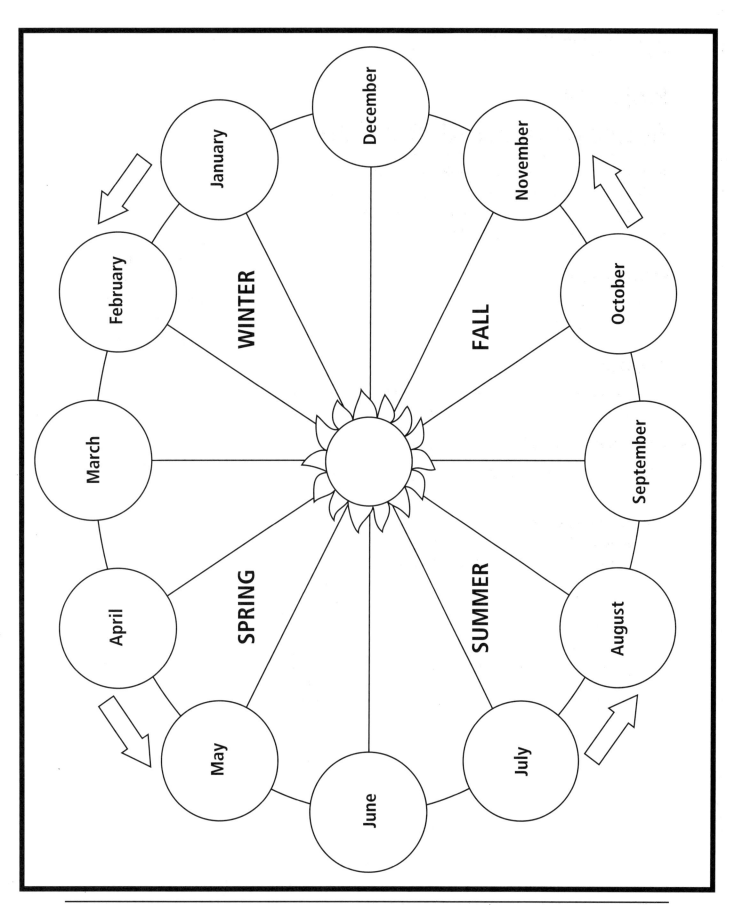

B. Procedure

1. Make the sun and its stand. To do this, turn one of the plastic cups upside down. Lay the flashlight sideways on the flat bottom of the cup. The "on" switch of the flashlight should face up. Tape the flashlight in place on the cup. The light from the flashlight will be like rays of sunlight. Have an adult use the bread knife to cut a slot out of the bottom of the 5" Styrofoam ball so that the ball fits easily over the flashlight. The ball represents the sun.

2. Make the Earth and its stand. Turn another plastic cup upside down. Glue the 2½" Styrofoam ball onto the flat bottom of the cup.

3. Paint the sun and Earth Styrofoam balls.

4. To show Earth's North Pole on the model, lightly mark the center top of the Earth ball with a pencil point. Measure ½" over to one side of this mark and make a second mark with your pencil. Push the push pin into this second mark for the North Pole. At this location on the ball, the pole should be about 23.5 degrees off center. To show Earth's equator on the model, slip the rubber band over the Earth ball. Adjust the rubber band so it is slanted on the ball and the push pin is centered above its widest point. The rubber band will be slanted compared to the cup stand. See the illustration of Earth's tilt on its axis (page 74).

5. Turn the Earth ball cup so the North Pole push pin is pointing up to the right and the equator rubber band is slanting downward to the right. With the laundry marker, write "Earth" on the side of the cup that now faces you.

6. If you'd like, color the photocopy of the "Seasons around the Sun" pattern. Then place the pattern on a table in front of you, with the words facing you so you can read them.

7. Place the Styrofoam Earth on one of the month circles on the seasons around the sun pattern. *The "Earth" label on the clear cup stand should face you for every month because this is how the actual Earth is tilted.* Move the earth from month to month around the pattern in a counterclockwise direction. During what month does the North Pole face away from the sun? What season begins during this month? During what month does the North Pole face the sun? What season begins during this month? Where does the North Pole face during March and September, and what seasons start with these months? Place the Earth on whatever the month is today. Where does the North Pole face, and what season is it?

8. Place the Styrofoam-and-flashlight sun on the "sun" location in the middle of the "Seasons around the Sun" pattern. Darken the room and turn on the flashlight. Move the Styrofoam Earth from month to month. *Be sure the "Earth" label on the cup always faces you and the North Pole points up and to the right.* As you move the earth from month to month, turn the flashlight so it is always shining on the earth. Where does the sun shine on the earth for each season? During what season does the sun shine directly on the Northern Hemisphere?

5. **Do the experiment.** While you do the activity, keep notes on what you do, including things you observe and discover.

6. **Write the conclusion.** Summarize what happened during the experiment. Was your hypothesis correct? How does the earth's tilt create the different seasons? What do you think would happen if the earth didn't tilt? What would you do differently if you did the experiment again?

7. **Share your findings.** Create a science project display to show what you have learned from doing the experiment. Check the rules for your own school's science fair to find out the exact requirements for your display. An idea for a display is on page 7.

Background Information: The Seasons

Each day, the Earth spins around on its axis. But the axis is not perfectly vertical. It is tilted 23.5 degrees. Earth remains at this same tilt as it revolves around the sun each year. It is this tilt that causes the different seasons.

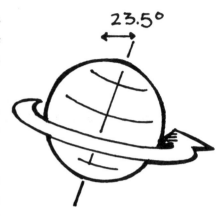

When the Northern Hemisphere has winter, the North Pole is tilted *away* from the sun. Less sunlight hits directly on the Northern Hemisphere, so the weather is cooler. Winter starts around December 21 and ends around March 21.

During spring, the North Pole is tipped sideways to the sun. Spring starts around March 21 and ends with the start of summer around June 21.

When the Northern Hemisphere has summer, the North Pole is tilted *toward* the sun. More sunlight hits directly on the Northern Hemisphere, so the weather is warmer. Summer starts around June 21 and ends around September 21.

During fall—like spring—the North Pole is tipped sideways to the sun. Fall starts around September 21 and ends with the start of winter on December 21.

When the Northern Hemisphere has winter, the Southern Hemisphere has summer. When the Northern Hemisphere has summer, the Southern Hemisphere has winter.

Extension

Find out about these yearly seasonal events: winter solstice, summer solstice, spring (or vernal) equinox, and autumnal equinox. On what dates do these events take place during the current year?

Category: **Science and Technology**
Topic: **Design a product**

Project 15:
Design a Product

National Science Education Standards: Science and Technology, Content Standard E: Abilities of Technological Design ("Identify appropriate problems for the technological design;" "Design a solution or product;" "Implement a proposed design;" "Communicate the process of technological design.") and Understanding about Science and Technology ("Perfectly designed solutions do not exist...")

* Information Sources

Visit your library and find books about inventions to see what other people have created. One suggested book is *Great Inventions*, with Richard Wood, consulting editor (New York: Barnes and Noble Books, 2003.) You can search the Internet by typing in this keyword: inventions.

Introduction

With this project, you get to invent a product.

A good way to do this project is to invent a product that will help you with your own everyday tasks. Your tasks might have to do with such things as communication, transportation, house work, school work, gardening, farming, or health and safety. By inventing a product for one of your own everyday tasks, you already know what does and doesn't work for you. Here are some steps you can follow.

Experiment

1. **List your problems.** Write down the tasks you do each day. For each task, list specific problems you have when doing it. For example, if the task is cleaning your teeth, the problem might be remembering to also floss. If the task is doing homework, the problem might be how to do it while you're on a long bus ride home from school.

2. **Pick one problem.** Pick just one of the problems in Step 1 that seems most interesting to you and one that could be solved with some type of new product. Write the problem out as a question. For example, you might ask, "How can I remember to floss when I brush my teeth?" Or, "How can I do homework on the bus?"

3. **List possible products.** Imagine new kinds of products that could help solve your problem so you can do the task more easily, quickly, safely, or comfortably. The products can be totally new and original. They can also be existing products that you change or improve upon. Think of as many product ideas as you can. Write out your ideas and draw quick sketches of them. For example, one product idea for cleaning your teeth might be a toothbrush that also flosses your teeth while you brush. A product idea for doing homework on the bus might be a backpack with a flap that folds out into a sturdy desk.

4. **Pick one product.** Pick your best product idea from Step 3.

5. **Do some research.** Read books about inventions or check the Internet to find out if a product like yours already exists. Ask people you know if they have the same kind of problem to see if your product might also help others. Also see Information Sources.

6. **Design the product.** Think of exactly what the product would look like, what materials it would be made out of, and how it would work. Write down your ideas and make detailed drawings of the product.

7. **Build a prototype.** Build a model or prototype of your product to show people what your invention looks like. If possible, try to build it from materials you already have. If your product has a motor or other moving parts, it is not necessary to include them on your model. While you build the model, keep notes on what you do, including things you observe and discover.

8. **Test your prototype.** If the prototype is a product that actually works, test it out to see if it solves your problem. Keep notes on your tests.

9. **Write your conclusion.** Study the prototype you built. Does it seem to solve your problem? Why or why not? Why is your product better than similar products that already exist? What are some possible bad points about your product? How would you change your product? What kinds of people might want to buy your product? What other kinds of products might also solve your problem?

10. **Share your findings.** Create a science project display to show what you have learned from creating your product. Be sure to display your prototype. Check the rules for your own school's science fair to find out the exact requirements for your display. An idea for a display is on page 7.

Extension

Find out about how to get a patent on an invention. A patent is a legal paper that gives the inventor the right to make or sell a product. Visit the Web site for the United States Patent and Trademark Office (USPTO) at www.uspto.gov.

Category: **Science in Personal and Social Perspectives**
Topic: **Disease prevention**

Project 16:
Wash Your Hands!

National Science Education Standards: Science in Personal and Social Perspectives, Content Standard F: Personal Health ("…Safe living involves the development and use of safety precautions and the recognition of risk in personal decisions.") and Risks and Benefits ("Students should understand the risks associated with…biological hazards (…viruses, bacterial, and parasites.")

Introduction

With this project, you'll experiment with several hand-washing products on apples to see which ones are most effective in cleaning—and helping stop the spread of some infectious diseases.

Experiment

1. **Ask a question.** Which product is most effective in stopping the spread of infectious diseases: regular bar soap, antibacterial soap, rubbing alcohol, or another cleanser of your choice?

2. **Research the topic.** See Information Sources.

3. **Formulate a hypothesis.** What do you think? Write your own hypothesis.

4. **Plan the experiment.**
   A. **Materials**

   five fresh, healthy-looking apples that are the same type and size
   one rotting apple (hit a fresh apple on the floor, make slices in it with a knife, and then seal it in a plastic bag and set it in a warm, dark location for a week; or ask a worker at your local grocery store for a rotten apple from the produce section)
   six pairs of plastic gloves
   paper plate

   plastic wrap
   five clear-plastic zipper-lock sandwich bags
   laundry marking pen
   tap water, warm
   regular bar soap
   paper towels
   antibacterial soap
   rubbing alcohol
   cotton ball
   your choice of another cleanser

* Information Sources

Visit your library and find books about infectious diseases and how they spread. One suggested book is *DK Eyewitness Books: Epidemic* by Brian Ward (New York: Dorling Kindersley, 2000). Look in consumer magazines to see which hand-washing products they've tested and feel are the most effective. You can search the Internet by typing in this keyword: infectious diseases. Also read the Background Information about infectious diseases and preventing them on page 80 of this book.

B. Procedure

1. The rotting apple will be the source of disease-causing organisms. Put on a pair of plastic gloves. Hold the rotting apple and thoroughly rub it all over the five fresh apples. Make sure the bad parts of the rotting apple touch the fresh apples. Throw away the rotting apple and the gloves. Set the five apples on a paper plate. Cover them with plastic wrap, and let them sit in a warm place for about 30 minutes.

2. Use the laundry marker to label the five plastic sandwich bags. On the first bag, write "#1: diseased and unwashed." On the second bag, write "#2: diseased and washed with soap and warm water." On the third bag, write "#3: diseased and washed with antibacterial soap and warm water." On the fourth bag, write "#4: diseased and washed with rubbing alcohol." And on the last bag, write "#5: diseased and washed with..." then fill in with the name of the cleanser you chose to use.

3. After 30 minutes, uncover the apples. Put on another pair of plastic gloves. Seal one of the five apples inside plastic bag #1. Throw out the gloves. This apple is your control object—the one object you don't change. You'll compare this unwashed control apple to the other test apples at the end of the experiment. The rest of the bags of apples will contain your experimental group—the objects you will perform tests on. The things you'll be testing on the apples, like soap and water, are called the independent variables.

4. Put on another pair of gloves. Wash one of the four remaining diseased apples with regular bar soap and warm tap water. Thoroughly dry the apple with paper towels. Immediately seal this apple in bag #2. Throw out the gloves.

5. Put on another pair of gloves. Wash another apple with antibacterial soap and warm tap water. Dry the apple and seal it in bag #3. Throw out the gloves.

6. Put on another pair of gloves. Dip the cotton ball in rubbing alcohol and rub the cotton all over another apple. Let the apple air dry for a minute, and then seal it in bag #4. Throw out the gloves.

7. Put on another pair of gloves. Wash the remaining apple in the cleanser of your choice. You can also use water to help wash this apple, if you choose. Dry the apple and seal it in bag #5. Throw away the gloves.

8. Place the five plastic bags of apples in a warm, dark location. Don't touch them for about two weeks. When the two weeks are up, study the apples and compare them. *Caution: Do not take the apples out of the plastic bags!*

5. Do the experiment. While you do the experiment, keep notes on what you do, including things you observe and discover. Record the results of your tests on a table like the one shown below.

Bag #	Type of Group (check one)		Independent variable (what was changed; write what you used to wash the diseased apple)	Condition of apple at end of experiment (write what the apple looked like after two weeks)
	Control (won't change)	Experimental (will change)		
1	X		nothing	
2		X	bar soap & warm water	
3				
4				
5				

6. Write the conclusion. Summarize what happened during the experiment. Was your hypothesis correct? Why or why not? What would you do differently if you did the experiment again?

7. Share your findings. Create a science project display to show what you have learned from doing your experiment. Check the rules for your own school's science fair to find out the exact requirements for your display. An idea for a display is on page 7.

Background Information:
Infectious Diseases and Preventing Them

Infectious diseases are diseases that can spread from one person to another. Infectious diseases can be caused by such things as a virus, bacterium, or fungus.

A virus is a microscopic organism that is made up of genetic material and depends upon living cells for survival. Viruses cause such diseases as the common cold, the flu, viral pneumonia, measles, rabies, polio, and AIDS.

Bacterium (bacterium is the singular form of bacteria) is an organism that is larger than a virus. Many kinds of bacteria are useful. But some kinds can cause diseases like pinkeye, strep throat, bacterial pneumonia, tuberculosis, and typhoid fever.

A fungus is a type of plant that doesn't have flowers, leaves, or roots and lives off living or dead things. A fungus grows best in a warm, moist area that is dark. A beneficial type of fungus is used in making antibiotics, which kill bacteria and help fight some diseases. But some funguses cause diseases such as athlete's foot.

Infectious diseases can spread when an infected person sneezes or shares a drinking glass with someone. Diseases can also spread when people touch each other, including touching hands. Some diseases can live on door knobs, telephones, pencils, and pens, so when someone touches those objects, they can get the infectious disease.

When people become infected, their bodies work to fight off the disease. Some medicines can also help. But preventing the spread of diseases is one of the best solutions.

An effective way to stop the spread of some infectious diseases is through washing hands. If people, including those with diseases, washed their hands often, it could help slow the spread of some infectious diseases like colds.

Some hand-washing cleansers are more effective than others in helping to stop the spread of diseases. Do this activity to find out which ones work the best.

Extension

Doctors have to be especially careful about spreading infectious diseases. Find out what hand-washing methods and products doctors use to keep their hands clean.

Category: Physical Science
Topic: Periodic Table of the Elements

Project 17:
Build a Periodic Table of the Elements

National Science Education Standards: Physical Science, Content Standard B: Properties and Changes of Matter ("There are more than 100 known elements that combine in a multitude of ways to produce compounds, which account for the living and nonliving substances that we encounter." "Substances are often placed in categories or groups if they react in similar ways; metals is an example of such a group.")

Introduction

With this project, you'll build a colorful model of the periodic table of the elements.

Activity

1. **Ask a question.** Where are the metal elements and where are the non-metal elements found on the period table of the elements?

2. **Research the topic.** See Information Sources.

3. **Plan the activity.**
    A. Materials
        one photocopy of the Periodic Table of the Elements pattern (page 83), enlarged and printed on 11" x 17" paper
        one sheet of 11" x 17" white construction paper
        scissors
        glue
        ruler
        construction paper, two different colors, any size
        pencil
        pen

* Information Sources

Visit your library and find books about the periodic table of the elements. One suggested book is *Chemistry* by Dr. Ann Newmark (New York: Dorling Kindersley, 1993). You can search the Internet by typing in this keyword: periodic table of the elements. Visit www.chemicalelements.com. Also read the Background Information about the periodic table of the elements on page 84 of this book.

B. Procedure

1. Cut out the photocopied periodic table pattern. Glue the periodic table onto the white sheet of construction paper.

2. With the ruler, measure one of the small rectangular spaces on the periodic table. Draw 22 rectangles about this same size (or slightly smaller) on one color of construction paper. These will be the non-metal elements. Near the top of each of these 22 colored rectangles, write these atomic numbers: 1, 2, 5, 6, 7, 8, 9, 10, 14, 15, 16, 17, 18, 33, 34, 35, 36, 52, 53, 54, 85, and 86.

3. Draw 90 rectangles of that same size on a different color of construction paper. These will be the metal elements. Near the top of each of these rectangles, write these atomic numbers: 3, 4, 11, 12, 13, 19 through 32, 37 through 51, 55 through 84, and 87 through 112.

4. Cut out all the colored rectangles from Step 1 and Step 2. Combine the two colors of rectangles and put them in order of atomic number from 1 through 112.

5. Set out the periodic table pattern you prepared in Step 1. Place the colored element rectangles in atomic number order from left to right on the spaces of the table. Some of the atomic numbers are written in on the table to help you. All of the element names are written in. Note: Elements 57 through 71 are grouped in a row at the bottom of the table because they have similar properties. These elements are called the lanthanides. Elements 89 through 103 are the actinides, and they are all radioactive.

6. When all the colored element rectangles are placed correctly on the table, glue them down. Put a line of glue only along the top of each of the colored element rectangles. That way, when the glue is dry, the rectangle will open like a flap to show the element name below it on the table.

7. On the colored rectangles, just below the atomic numbers, write in the symbol for each element. Use the Table of Atomic Numbers and Symbols shown in Background Information to help you.

4. **Do the activity.** While you do the activity, keep notes on what you do, including things you observe and discover. Where are the metal elements on the table? Where are the non-metals? Can you look at a symbol and figure out the element name under the flap? How many element names are familiar to you?

Name: _____

Periodic Table
of the Elements

1																	2
Hydrogen																	Helium
Lithium	4											5			8		10
	Beryllium											Boron	Carbon	Nitrogen	Oxygen	Flourine	Neon
Sodium	12											Aluminum	Silicon	15			
	Magnesium													Phosphorus	Sulfur	Chlorine	Argon
Potassium	20	Scandium	Titanium	Vanadium	Chromium	Manganese	Iron	27	Nickel	Copper	Zinc	Gallium	Germanium	Arsenic	Selenium	35	Krypton
	Calcium	39						Cobalt	46							Bromine	
Rubidium	56	Yttrium	72	Niobium	Molybdenum	Technetium	Ruthenium	Rhodium	Palladium	79	Cadmium	Indium	Tin	Antimony	Tellurium	Iodine	Xenon
55	Strontium		Zirconium							Silver					84		
Cesium	88	57	Hafnium	Tantalum	Tungsten	Rhenium	Osmium	Iridium	Platinum	Gold	Mercury	Thallium	Lead	Bismuth	Polonium	Astatine	Radon
Berium	Radium	Lanthanum	105	Dubrium	Seaborngium	Bohrium	Hassium	Meitnerium	Darmstadtium	Element 111	112						
Francium	89		Rutherfordium								Element 112						
	Actinium																

Lanthanide series

57	Cerium	Praseodymium	Neodymium	Promethium	Samarium	Europium	Gadolinium	Terbium	Dysprosium	Holmium	Erbium	Thulium	Ytterbium	71
Lanthanum														

Actinide series

89	Thorium	Protactinium	Uranium	Neptunium	Plutonium	95	Curium	Barkelium	Californium	Einsteinium	Fermium	Mendelevium	102	Lawrencium
Actinium						Americium							Nobelium	

Background Information:
Periodic Table of the Elements

Elements are pure substances that cannot be broken down further into any other kind of pure substance. Gold is an example of an element. If you keep breaking down gold, you get smaller and smaller particles of gold.

All elements are made up of just one kind of atom. An atom is the smallest particle of an element. Gold is made up of gold atoms. Oxygen, another element, is made up of oxygen atoms.

Atoms contain positively-charged particles called protons. Each element has a different number of protons. Gold has 79 protons, and oxygen has 8.

The number of protons in an element is the element's atomic number. The atomic number for gold is 79 because it has 79 protons. Oxygen has 8 protons, so its atomic number is 8. The element with the lowest atomic number is hydrogen, which has an atomic number of 1. More elements may be discovered, but today there are 112 known elements. This means the highest atomic number is 112.

The periodic table of the elements is a table that shows all 112 elements arranged in order of atomic number. In addition to the atomic number, the table shows the name of the element along with its symbol. The symbol for gold is Au, which stands for the Latin name of gold, *aurum*. Like gold, many other symbols on the periodic table are based on the Latin names of the elements.

Elements with similar properties are arranged together on the table. On one part of the table is a group of elements called metals. Metals are shiny and can conduct electricity. Gold is an example of a metal. The other part of the table has elements without these properties, and they are called non-metals. Oxygen is a non-metal.

Extension

Find out which of the elements make up Earth's crust. What elements are found in our atmosphere? Your body is also made up of elements; what are they?

Atomic number	Symbol	Atomic number	Symbol	Atomic number	Symbol	Atomic number	Symbol
1	H	29	Cu	57	La	85	At
2	He	30	Zn	58	Ce	86	Rn
3	Li	31	Ga	59	Pr	87	Fr
4	Be	32	Ge	60	Nd	88	Ra
5	B	33	As	61	Pm	89	Ac
6	C	34	Se	62	Sm	90	Th
7	N	35	Br	63	Eu	91	Pa
8	O	36	Kr	64	Gd	92	U
9	F	37	Rb	65	Tb	93	Np
10	Ne	38	Sr	66	Dy	94	Pu
11	Na	39	Y	67	Ho	95	Am
12	Mg	40	Zr	68	Er	96	Cm
13	Al	41	Nb	69	Tm	97	Bk
14	Si	42	Mo	70	Yb	98	Cf
15	P	43	Tc	71	Lu	99	Es
16	S	44	Ru	72	Hf	100	Fm
17	Cl	45	Rh	73	Ta	101	Md
18	Ar	46	Pd	74	W	102	No
19	K	47	Ag	75	Re	103	Lr
20	Ca	48	Cd	76	Os	104	Rf
21	Sc	49	In	77	Ir	105	Db
22	Ti	50	Sn	78	Pt	106	Sg
23	V	51	Sb	79	Au	107	Bh
24	Cr	52	Te	80	Hg	108	Hs
25	Mn	53	I	81	Tl	109	Mt
26	Fe	54	Xe	82	Pb	110	Ds
27	Co	55	Cs	83	Bi	111	Uuu
28	Ni	56	Ba	84	Po	112	Uub

Category: Physical Science
Topic: Molecules

Project 18:
Gumdrop Molecules

National Science Education Standards: Physical Science, Content Standard B: Properties and Changes of Properties in Matter ("Substances react chemically in characteristic ways with other substances to form new substances (compounds) with different characteristic properties.")

Introduction

With this project, you'll make models of different molecules.

Activity

1. **Ask a question.** How can you show the atoms that make up the molecules of different compounds?

2. **Research the topic.** See Information Sources.

3. **Plan the activity.**
   ### A. Materials
   gumdrop candies in many different colors
   hole punch
   toothpicks (round style)
   paper clips
   3" x 5" cards
   information about the compounds
   scissors

> ### *Information Sources
> Visit your library and find books about matter and molecules. Two suggested books are *The Way Science Works* by Robin Kerrod and Dr. Sharon Ann Holgate (New York: DK Publishing, 2002) and *Eyewitness Books: Chemistry* by Dr. Ann Newmark (New York: Dorling Kindersley, 1993). You can search the Internet by typing in this keyword: molecule. Also read the Background Information about molecules on page 88 of this book.

B. Procedure

1. Put at least eight different gumdrop molecules together. The gumdrops are the atoms. The toothpicks are the bonds that join them together. For example, to make the water molecule, select one color of gumdrop, such as blue, to be the oxygen atom. Select two gumdrops of the same color, such as red, to be the two hydrogen atoms. Push two toothpicks into each side of the oxygen gumdrop. Stick a hydrogen gumdrop on the empty ends of the toothpicks. Use the Table of Twelve Common Compounds and Their Molecules in the Background Information for ideas for other molecules. You might always use the same color of gumdrop for one particular type of atom for all your molecules. For example, you might always use a red gumdrop for hydrogen and a blue gumdrop for oxygen. *Be careful of the sharp points on the toothpicks!*

2. Label each molecule. To do this, make tags by cutting the 3" x 5" cards in half lengthwise to make 3" x 2½" cards. Punch a hole in one end of the tag. On the front of the tag, write the compound's name and the chemical formula for its molecule. Find out about the compound for the molecule—look in a dictionary, encyclopedia, a science book, or on the Internet. Then on the back of the tag, write a sentence that explains what the compound is. Attach the tag to the molecule by pushing a paper clip through the punched hole in the tag. Slip the other end of the paper clip over one of the toothpicks on the molecule.

4. **Do the activity.** While you do the experiment, keep notes on what you do, including things you observe and discover. Make a table of the molecules you made from the gumdrops like the one shown below.

	Name of compound	Chemical formula	Information about the chemical
1.			
2.			
3.			
4.			
5.			
6.			
7.			
8.			

Background Information: Molecules

Atoms are the tiniest particles in matter that can exist alone. The center core of the atom is the nucleus, which contains positively-charged particles called protons. Moving in the space around the nucleus are negatively-charged particles called electrons. Usually, the number of protons in a particular atom is equal to the number of electrons in that atom. This means the positive charges balance the negative charges, so the atom has no charge.

Elements are pure substances that cannot be broken down further into any other kind of pure substance. There are 112 known elements on Earth. Each element contains just one kind of atom. The element hydrogen is made up of only hydrogen atoms. The element oxygen is made up of only oxygen atoms.

Two or more atoms can bond together to form molecules. The atoms bond together in a molecule because their atoms share electrons. This type of bond is called a covalent bond.

Molecules make up substances called compounds. Two hydrogen atoms and one oxygen atom bond together to form a certain molecule. This molecule makes up the compound, water. Eight sulfur atoms combine to form a molecule that makes up the compound, sulfur.

Scientists have created symbols to stand for each element. The symbol for hydrogen is H. The symbol for oxygen is O. H_2O means two hydrogen atoms and one oxygen atom. If no number is written after an element in the formula, it means there is just one atom. The symbol for sulfur is S, so S_8 means eight sulfur atoms. Many symbols are based on Latin names. For example, the symbol for lead is Pb, which stands for *plumbum*, the Latin name for lead.

Extension

Find out more about the covalent bonds that hold molecules together. How does a covalent bond compare to an ionic bond?

TABLE OF SIX COMMON MOLECULES

Name of compound	Chemical formula	Atoms in formula	Diagram
	H_2O	2 hydrogen 1 oxygen	
carbon monoxide	CO	1 carbon 1 oxygen	
carbon dioxide	CO_2	1 carbon 2 oxygen	
chlorine	Cl_2	2 chlorine	
ammonia	NH_3	1 nitrogen 3 hydrogen	
sulfur dioxide	SO_2	1 sulfur 2 oxygen	

Category: Physical Science
Topic: Properties of Water

Project 19:
Presto Change-O Water

Information Sources

Visit your library and find books about water and the states of matter. One suggested book is *The Way Science Works* by Robin Kerrod and Dr. Sharon Ann Holgate (New York: DK Publishing, 2002). You can search the Internet by typing in these keywords: water and three states of matter. Also read the Background Information about the three states of matter on page 93 of this book.

National Science Education Standards: Physical Science, Content Standard B: Properties and Changes of Properties in Matter ("A substance has characteristic properties, such as density, a boiling point, and solubility.") and Transfer of Energy ("Energy is a property of many substances and is associated with heat…energy is transferred in many ways.")

Introduction

With this project, you'll explore the three states of matter for water.

Activity

1. **Ask a question.** What are the three states of matter for water?

2. **Research the topic.** See Information Sources.

3. **Plan the activity.**
   A. Materials
      metal pie tin
      thermometer
      several tin cans with labels removed
      ice cubes
      water
      paper towels
      measuring cup
      laundry marker
      one 10-ounce (296 ml) clear plastic disposable drinking cup
      plastic sandwich bag
      rubber band
      freezer
      optional: small metal pot, candy thermometer, ruler, and stove or hot plate

B. Procedure

1. First capture invisible water vapor gas from the air and make it visible as liquid water. To do this, set the metal pie plate in a warm location. Fill the tin cans with ice cubes. Then fill each can with tap water so that the ice cubes don't rise above the tops of the cans. Use the paper towels to thoroughly dry the outsides of the cans. Carefully set the cans in the metal pie plate so you don't spill any water. Observe the outside of the cans. After an hour, observe the outside of the cans again. Is there any difference? Is there water in the pie tin? How did it get there if none of the water from the cans spilled? Water vapor from the air cooled and condensed on the outside of the cans, and then it dripped into the pan. Remove the tin cans from the pie plate, being careful not to spill any water from the cans. Pour the water from the pie tin into a measuring cup. You will need about ⅓ of a cup of water for the next step, so you might need to repeat step 1 in order to capture more water vapor from the air (or you can simply add tap water to the liquid water to make ⅓ cup.) Pour the ⅓ cup water into the clear plastic drinking cup. Set a thermometer in the water for two minutes, and then record this temperature. Use a laundry marker to mark the level of the water on the plastic cup. Write "Step 1" next to this mark.

2. Turn the liquid water from Step 1 into solid ice. To do this, leave the thermometer in the water, and cover the thermometer and the cup with the plastic bag. Seal the bag on the cup with a rubber band to help keep the water from spilling. Set the cup in a freezer over night. The next day, record the temperature of the ice. Draw a mark on the cup to mark the level of the ice, and write "Step 2" next to it. Is the level the same as it was when the water was still a liquid at the end of Step 1?

3. Turn the solid ice back into liquid water. Remove the plastic bag from the cup. Set the cup, with the thermometer still inside it, in a warm location until the ice is completely melted. Record the temperature of the liquid water. Draw a mark on the cup to show the level of the water and write "Step 3" next to it. Is the level different this time?

4. Finally, turn the liquid water back into water vapor. Leave the thermometer in the cup and set the cup in a warm, sunny window for two weeks. After the two weeks, draw a mark on the cup to show the level of the water, and write "Step 4" next to it. Where did some of this water go? Record the temperature of the water.

---

5. Optional: Speed up evaporation of the liquid water by boiling it. To do this, save the remaining water from Step 4 and pour it into a metal pot. Clip a candy thermometer to the side of the pot so its temperature sensor bulb sits in the water. Use a ruler to measure the level of the water in the pot. Have an adult set the pot on a stove or hotplate and bring the water to a boil. Let it boil for about five minutes. Record the temperature of the water. Remove the pot from the stove and let it cool for about ten minutes. Being careful not to burn yourself with the water or the pot, measure the level of the water now. Where did this water go?

4. **Do the activity.** While you do the experiment, keep notes on what you do, including things you observe and discover. For each step in the experiment, record information about the state of water at the beginning of the step, the process change, and the state of the water at the end of the step. Use a table like the one shown below.

Step #	Start of step	Process change during step (check one)					End of step		Water level (check one)	
	State of water	Condensation	Freezing	Melting	Evaporation	Boiling	State of water	Temperature	Higher	Lower
1	vapor	X					liquid		///	///
2	liquid						ice			
3	ice						liquid			
4	liquid						vapor			
5 (optional)	liquid						vapor			

Background Information:
Matter and Its Three States

Matter is anything that takes up space. All matter is made up of tiny particles called atoms. Atoms can combine to form larger particles called molecules. Atoms and molecules move about in matter.

The three states of matter are solid, liquid, and gas. Atoms and molecules move about at different rates in each of the states. In a solid, the atoms and molecules don't move much because they are closely bonded together. This means the solid keeps its shape. In a liquid, the atoms and molecules move about in all directions, so the liquid can flow into any shape. In a gas, there is a lot of space, so the atoms and molecules have room to move about in all directions. Gases do not have a definite shape, and they usually can't be seen, touched, or smelled.

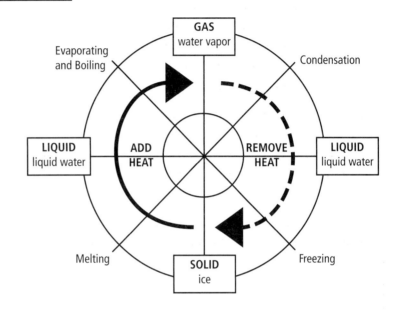

Matter can change state. This happens when heat energy is added or removed from it. To change a solid into a liquid, heat energy is added to the solid so that the atoms and molecules move faster. This process is called melting.

To change a liquid into a gas, heat energy is added to the liquid so its atoms and molecules move even faster. This process is called evaporation. If a lot of heat energy is added to the liquid through boiling, the liquid will evaporate even faster.

To change a gas back into a liquid, heat energy is taken away from the gas so it cools. This process is called condensation.

To change a liquid back into a solid, more heat energy is taken away from the liquid so it cools. This process is called freezing.

Water can occur in all three states of matter. When water is in the solid state, it is called ice. When water freezes, it does something unusual for a solid; it expands and becomes lighter. Most other substances become heavier or denser when they turn into solids. Because ice becomes lighter, it is able to float in water. In the liquid state, water is simply called water or liquid water. In the gas state, water is invisible and is called water vapor.

Extension

Find out about other substances and what they are like in the three different states.

Category: Physical Science
Topic: Electromagnetic Spectrum

Project 20:
Touring the Electromagnetic Spectrum

National Science Education Standards: Physical Science, Content Standard B: Transfer of Energy ("Energy is a property of many substances…" and "energy is transferred in many ways.")

Introduction

With this project, you'll "tour" the electromagnetic spectrum by making a model of it.

Activity

1. **Ask a question.** What waves make up the electromagnetic spectrum and what order do the waves appear on it?

2. **Research the topic.** See Information Sources.

3. **Plan the activity.**
   ### A. Materials
   three letter-size manila file folders
   scissors
   tape
   one photocopy of the electromagnetic spectrum pattern (page 95), enlarged and printed on white 8½" by 11" paper
   six different colors of 9" x 12" construction paper (not white)
   glue
   one small rectangle of white construction paper, about ½" x 1"
   crayons or colored pencils
   magazine pictures of different objects that use electromagnetic waves (such as a microwave oven, televisions, satellite dish, and an X-ray machine)

* Information Sources

Visit your library and find books about the electromagnetic spectrum. One suggested book is *The Usborne Internet-Linked Science Encyclopedia* by Kirsteen Rogers, et al. (England: Usborne Publishing Ltd, 2002). You can search the Internet by typing in this keyword: electromagnetic spectrum. Check out the NASA Web site with information about the electromagnetic spectrum at imagers.gsfc.nasa.gov/ems. Also read the Background Information about the electromagnetic spectrum on pages 97–98 of this book.

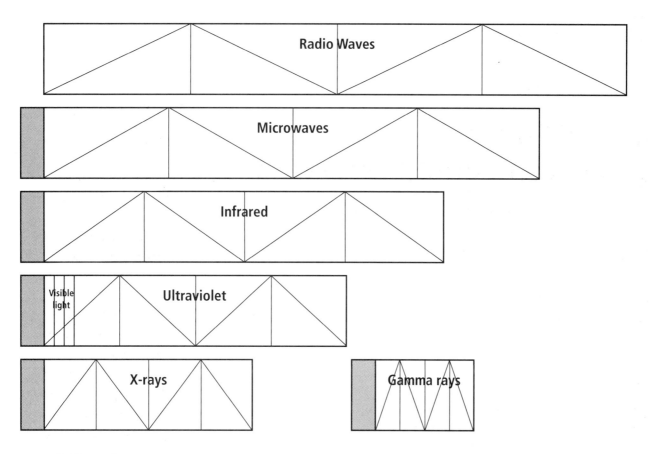

B. Procedure

1. Prepare the background for the electromagnetic spectrum using the file folders. If there are tabs on the file folders, use the scissors to cut off the tabs so that the edges of the file folders are straight across. Lay one of the closed file folders flat on the table with its fold away from you. Measure half way across the cover of the folder lengthwise and draw a line. Fold back the cover along this line. Open up the folded cover of the file folder so that it stands up like a short wall. The back of the file folder should rest flat against the table like a floor. Repeat with the other two file folders. Set the three prepared file folders side by side, short edges together, so they overlap about ½ inch. Tape them together at the overlapping edges.

2. Cut around the six rectangles on the electromagnetic spectrum pattern and throw out the excess paper. Glue the rectangles together end-to-end at the tabs to make one long strip. They should be in this order from left to right: radio waves, microwaves, infrared radiation, ultraviolet radiation (including visible light), x-rays, and gamma rays. Set the long strip along the "short wall" of the file folders, with the bottom of the strip at the crease. Tape the strip in place.

3. Choose a color of construction paper to represent radio waves. Measure a 2-inch strip down one long edge of the construction paper. Cut the strip out and fold it in half lengthwise so you have a colored strip that is one inch wide. Set the colored strip against the wave pattern for radio waves along the "short wall" of the file

folders. Crease an accordion-fold wave into the colored strip to match the shape of the radio waves on the pattern. Cut off any excess length of the colored strip and throw it away. Glue the colored wave to the "floor" of the cardboard near the crease so that the wave mirrors the radio wave pattern on the "short wall" just behind it. Repeat for the rest of the electromagnetic waves.

4. The small, white rectangle will be for the tiny visible light area of the spectrum. Use the crayons or colored pencils to draw parallel colored lines on the white rectangle. These lines represent the colors of the rainbow that make up visible light. The color red has the longest wavelength, so it is the first color on the left of the white rectangle. Continue drawing colored lines to the right of red in this order: orange, yellow, green, blue, and violet. At the beginning of the ultraviolet radiation wave, glue the white rectangle. Be sure the red line is on the side nearest the infrared wave, and the violet line is on the side nearest the ultraviolet radiation wave.

5. Write the names of the seven types of waves (including visible light) on the "floor" of the cardboard, just in front of the waves. In this same space, you can also glue on several magazine pictures of objects that represent the different types of waves. For example, you could show a picture of a microwave oven for microwaves and a television for radio waves. Note: The wavelengths used on this model are not to any scale. The model simply shows how the wavelengths grow shorter as you move along the spectrum. If the actual scale size of the waves was used on this model, the radio waves could be up to 100,000 meters long, while the gamma ray waves would be invisible because they are so tiny.

4. **Do the activity.** While you do the activity, keep notes on what you do, including things you observe and discover.

Background Information:
The Electromagnetic Spectrum

All forms of moving energy travel in waves. One type of wave is the electromagnetic wave. Electromagnetic waves are made up of vibrating electric charges. The vibrating electric charges create an alternating pattern of electrical fields and magnetic fields. Together, these fields form an electromagnetic wave.

Electromagnetic waves are transverse waves. This means that the particles vibrate at right angles to the direction in which the wave is moving. Electromagnetic waves can travel through most solids, liquids, and gases. They can also move through a vacuum where there is no matter. All electromagnetic waves move at the speed of light, which is 186,000 miles per second (300,000 kilometers per second). Most of the electromagnetic waves are invisible, except for a tiny area of visible light.

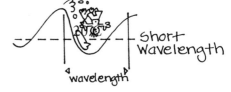

Electromagnetic waves form a regular pattern of crests and troughs. The distance between the crest of one wave and the crest of the following wave is called the wavelength. The greater the distance between the two crests, the longer the wavelength. Electromagnetic waves with the shortest wavelengths have the most energy.

There are seven main types of electromagnetic waves. All of them together make up the electromagnetic spectrum. The different types are arranged in order of wavelength. Radio waves have the longest wavelength and the least amount of energy. Gamma rays have the shortest wavelength and the greatest amount of energy.

Name: _____

Wave Type	Description	Approx. Wavelength Range (meters)	
		From	To
Radio waves	Waves with the longest wavelengths and the least amount of energy. They include radio and television broadcasting waves as well as satellite and cellular phone signals.	$\frac{1}{10}$	1,000
Microwaves	Used in radar for weather forecasting and microwave ovens.	$\frac{1}{100}$	$\frac{1}{10}$
Infrared radiation	Produced by things that are hot. The sun's rays travel to earth as infrared rays. Remote controls for TVs use infrared.	$\frac{7}{10,000,000}$	$\frac{1}{100}$
Visible light	This tiny region contains the only electromagnetic waves that people can see. People see visible light as the seven colors of the rainbow. Each color of visible light has a different wavelength. Red has the longest wavelength, while violet has the shortest wavelength.	$\frac{4}{10,000,000}$	$\frac{7}{10,000,000}$
Ultraviolet radiation	Ultraviolet radiation from the sun makes your skin burn or tan.	$\frac{1}{1,000,000,000}$	$\frac{4}{10,000,000}$
X-rays	X-rays are used in hospitals to make shadowed pictures of bones and in airports to see what is inside people's luggage.	$\frac{1}{100,000,000,000}$	$\frac{1}{1,000,000,000}$
Gamma rays	Gamma rays have so much energy that they can kill living cells, which is why they are used in hospitals to sterilize tools.	$\frac{1}{1,000,000,000,000}$	$\frac{1}{100,000,000,000}$

Extension

Find out about equipment that sends or receives the different kinds of electromagnetic waves. For example, how does a radio or television station broadcast radio waves? How does a radio or television receive the signal? How does a satellite dish, microwave oven, or X-ray machine work? What kind of hospital equipment makes gamma rays to sterilize tools?

Category: Life Science
Topic: Plant and Animal Cells

Project 21:
Plant and Animal Cells

National Science Education Standards. Life Science, Content Standard C: Structure and Function in Living Systems ("Living systems at all levels of organization demonstrate the complementary nature of structure and function. Important levels of organization for structure and function include cells…" and "All organisms are composed of cells—the fundamental unit of life" and "Cells carry on the many functions needed to sustain life" and "Specialized cells perform specialized functions in multi-cellular organisms.")

Introduction

With this project, you'll make a model of a plant cell and an animal cell.

Activity

1. **Ask a question.** What do plant cells look like and how do they compare to animal cells?

2. **Research the topic.** See Information Sources.

3. **Plan the activity.**
   A. Materials
   one large mixing bowl
   1-cup measuring cup
   7 cups of all-purpose flour
   1¾ cups salt
   2½ cups water
   mixing spoon
   optional: two 1-gallon zipper-lock plastic bags
   two 10-inch heavy paper plates or Styrofoam plates
   waxed paper
   paint brushes, one medium-sized and one small
   acrylic paints, non-toxic, in various colors (from craft store)

***Information Sources**
Visit your library and find books about cells. Two suggested books are *How Nature Works* by David Burnie (New York: The Reader's Digest Association, Inc., 1991) and *The Usborne Internet-Linked Science Encyclopedia* by Kirsteen Rogers, et al (London: Usborne Publishing Ltd, 2002). You can search the Internet by typing in these keywords: plant cells and animal cells. Also read the Background Information about cells on pages 102–103 of this book.

B. Procedure

1. Prepare the dough for the cell models. In one large mixing bowl, place the flour, salt, and water. Mix thoroughly with a spoon. When the dough becomes too thick to mix with a spoon, continue mixing and squeezing the dough with your hands. Work the dough with your hands for about ten minutes until it is well-blended and smooth. Divide the dough in half. Optional: You can store the dough for several weeks in the refrigerator now, if you wish. Put each half of the dough in a separate gallon zipper lock plastic bag, and put the bags in the refrigerator.

2. Tear off two square sheets of waxed paper and lay a sheet on each plate.

3. Make a model of a cross-section of a plant cell. Take one of the halves of dough from step 1. Pull off about one-third of the dough and set it aside. Place the remaining larger piece of dough on one of the plates you prepared in step 2. Use your hands to shape it like a brick that's about 4 inches wide, 6 inches long, and 1½ inches thick. Make a large indentation in the top of the cell for the *vacuole*. Use the smaller (one-third) piece of dough you set aside to make the other plant cell structures. For the *nucleus*, roll a chunk of the dough into a ball and press it into the plant cell. Roll several small pieces of dough into fat hotdogs for the *chloroplasts* and press them into the plant cell all around the vacuole. Make smaller hotdogs for the *mitochondria*. Roll dough into a long, thin snake and fold it back and forth on the dough near the nucleus. This is the *endoplasmic reticulum*. Use the illustration of a cross section of a typical plant cell in Background Information to help you make the model.

4. Make a model of a cross-section of an animal cell. Take the other half of dough from step 1. Pull off about one-third of the dough and set it aside. Place the larger piece of dough on one of the plates you prepared in step 2. Use your hands to shape it into a disk that's about 4 inches in diameter. As you did for the plant cell, use the smaller (one-third) piece of dough to make the other structures. After making a small ball for the *nucleus*, push it into the center of the animal cell. Make the *endoplasmic reticulum* and *mitochondria* like you did for the plant cell. Make several small *vacuoles* by pushing your finger into the dough of the animal cell. Use the illustration of a cross section of a typical animal cell in Background Information to help you make the model. Note: Your model plant and animal cells are not to scale; most real cells can only be seen with a microscope.

5. Leave your plant cell and animal cell models on the plates and set them in a warm, dry area to dry for at least 5 days.

6. Paint both your plant and animal cell models and their structures with the acrylic paint.

7. Make a key that shows the different parts of your plant cell and animal cell models. You can glue small numbers on the models, and then on a separate sheet of paper, list each number and what the name and function of the structure is for that number. Or you can make a sketch of each of the cells and name the parts and their functions directly on the sketches.

4. Do the activity. While you do the activity, keep notes on what you do, including things you observe and discover.

Background Information: Cells

A cell is the smallest unit that makes up an organism. An organism is any living thing, including plants and animals. A cell is like a miniature factory that carries on processes that help the organism live and reproduce. Reproduce means to make new plants and animals.

Some tiny organisms like bacteria have just one cell. But most plants and animals have many cells. These organisms are called multi-cellular organisms. All the cells that make up a multi-cellular organism work together to help the organism function.

The cells of a multi-cellular organism are usually specialized. A specialized cell does one specific job. In plants, for example, one kind of specialized cell makes up the outside of the leaf, while another kind makes up the inside of the leaf. In animals, specialized cells include skin cells, blood cells, and brain cells.

Plants are organisms that don't move around, so they cannot hunt for food to eat. Instead, plants make their own food. Through a process called photosynthesis, plants make food in their leaves using light from the sun, carbon dioxide from the air, and water from the soil. A main function of plant cells is to help the plant carry out photosynthesis.

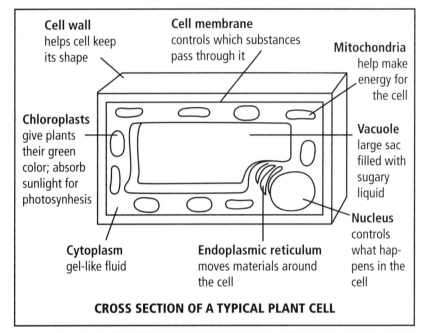

CROSS SECTION OF A TYPICAL PLANT CELL

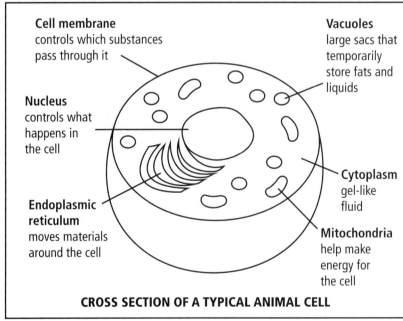

CROSS SECTION OF A TYPICAL ANIMAL CELL

Unlike plants, animals can move around, and they depend upon other organisms for food. Muscle cells help the animal move. Other cells help the animal digest food and turn it into energy.

Plant and animal cells both contain a nucleus, an endoplasmic reticulum, mitochondria, and cytoplasm. Both kinds of cells are also surrounded by a thin cell membrane, but plant and animal cells also have some differences.

Plant cells are usually rectangular. They have a thick cell wall that holds the cell in shape. Much of the plant cell is taken up by a large fluid-filled sac called a vacuole. Plant cells also have chloroplasts that trap sunlight to carry out photosynthesis.

Animal cells are usually spherical like a ball and are smaller than plant cells. They have no cell wall. Rather than one large vacuole, animal cells have a number of small vacuoles.

Extension

Use a microscope to observe real plant and animal cells.

Category: Life Science
Topic: Composting

Project 22:
Compost Jug

National Science Education Standards: Life Science, Content Standard C: Populations and Ecosystems ("A population consists of all individuals of a species that occur together at a given place and time. All populations living together and the physical factors with which they interact compose an ecosystem" and "Populations of organisms can be categorized by the function they serve in an ecosystem…producers…consumers…and decomposers…")

Introduction

With this project, you'll find out about decomposers and how they work by creating a miniature composter.

Activity

1. **Ask a question.** How can you make a composter that uses decomposers to turn dead plant matter into a nutritious soil called compost?

2. **Research the topic.** See Information Sources.

3. **Plan the activity.**
   ### A. Materials
      one 1-gallon plastic milk jug
      laundry marking pen
      sharp knife (for adult use only)
      scissors
      fresh kitchen scraps like apple peels, lettuce leaves, and
         orange peel (no meat, dairy, or egg products)
      fresh yard waste like grass clippings, flowers, and fresh leaves
      dry yard waste like straw, dry hay, dry weeds, and dry leaves
      several handfuls of fresh garden soil
      water
      thermometer

> ### *Information Sources
> Visit your library and find books about composting. One suggested book is *Popular Science Almanac* (New York: Popular Science for Kids Books, LLC, 2004). You can search the Internet by typing in these keywords: decomposers and compost piles. Also read the Background Information about composting on page 107 of this book.

B. Procedure

1. Use the laundry marker to draw an oval slightly larger than your hand near the top of the milk jug. Have an adult use the sharp knife to cut out the oval. The oval should be trimmed smooth with scissors so there aren't any sharp edges around it. Also have the adult use the point of the knife to make many random slices all around the sides of the jug. The oval hole and slices will help let air into the compost jug. Remove the plastic cap from the milk jug to provide more air.

2. Break or cut up both the fresh and dry materials into small pieces. Push the pieces into the jug through the oval hole. There should be about twice as much fresh material as dry material. The dry and fresh materials together should fill the jug so it is almost full.

3. Add dirt to the jug. Then add about an eighth of a cup of water. Gently shake the contents of the jug. This helps mix in the dirt and water. It also helps unpack the dry and fresh material so air can flow around.

4. Push a thermometer into the middle of the contents inside the compost jug.

5. Set the compost jug outside where animals cannot get into it. If it is hot outside, put the jug in a shady location. If it is cold outside, set it out in the sun. You can also put the compost jug indoors next to an open window where it gets plenty of fresh air but no direct sunlight.

6. Each day for at least three weeks, observe the contents of your compost jug. What do the contents look like? What things, if any, are starting to decompose? How does it smell? What is the temperature? Is the jug as full as it was when you started the project? How have things changed from the previous day and week?

7. Each week, gently shake the contents of the compost jug. A properly-functioning compost pile smells like fresh garden soil. If the contents of your compost jug start to smell badly, it might mean the helpful bacteria in it are not getting enough air or water. Try moving the jug to an area where it can get more air, or have an adult slash more holes in the side of the jug. If the contents of the jug are very dry, sprinkle on a little more water.

8. Optional: You might continue maintaining your compost jug after your project is finished. That way, you can see how the decomposers turn the contents into dirt-like compost called humus. This process can take many months. You can add more fresh and dry material, more soil, and/or more water to your compost jug, if you wish. Add the completed humus from your compost jug to a garden.

4. Do the activity. While you do the activity, keep notes on what you do, including things you observe and discover. Record the results of your daily observations of the compost jug on a table like the one shown below.

#	Date	Appearance	Smell	Temperature	Notes
1					
2					
3					
4					
5					
6					
7					
8					
9					
10					
11					
12					
13					
14					
15					
16					
17					
18					
19					
20					
21					

Background Information: Composting

An ecosystem is made up of all the organisms living in a particular area. An organism is any living thing, including plants and animals. An ecosystem also includes the physical features of the area, such as the air, water, and trees.

Each separate kind of organism living in the ecosystem is called a population. The different populations that make up a particular ecosystem depend upon each other for food. A food chain is a series of plants and animals in an ecosystem, each of which depends upon the one ahead of it for food.

At the beginning of the food chain are the producers. The producers are the plants. Plants make their own food, so they don't eat other organisms in the ecosystem.

Next in line in the food chain are the consumers. The consumers are the animals. Some animals eat plants, some eat other animals, and some eat both.

Bacteria

Decomposers are another important part of the food chain. Decomposers are nature's recyclers because they break down dead plants and animals. In the process, the decomposers create a nutritious soil called humus that plants can use.

Bacteria are the most common type of decomposer. Bacteria are microscopic, meaning you need a microscope to see them. There are many different kinds of bacteria. The second most common type of decomposer is fungi. Fungi include mushrooms, toadstools, mildew, and mold.

Fungi

Decomposers work naturally in the forest and other environments. But gardeners sometimes use the help of decomposers on purpose to create nutritious soil for their flowers and vegetables. Gardeners do this by making a compost pile in the garden. The main ingredients of a compost pile are soil, fresh plant material, dry plant material, air, and water. The soil provides millions of decomposers that break down the plant material. Air and water help the decomposers do their job. As the decomposers work, they can create a lot of heat—sometimes up to 130° Fahrenheit!

Extension

Visit a forest or other natural area. What populations of plants and animals are the producers and what are the consumers? Do you see any large decomposers like mushrooms, or can you see evidence that microscopic decomposers, like bacteria, are at work?

Category: Life Science
Topic: Extinction

Project 23:
Endangered Species Poster

National Science Education Standards: Life Science, Content Standard C: Diversity and Adaptations of Organisms ("Extinction of a species occurs when the environment changes and the adaptive characteristics of a species are insufficient to allow its survival. Fossils indicate that many organisms that lived long ago are extinct. Extinction of species is common; most of the species that have lived on the earth no longer exist.")

Introduction

With this project, you'll make a poster showing one type of animal that is currently endangered—meaning it is in danger of dying off or becoming extinct in the future.

Activity

1. **Ask a question.** What is one kind of present-day animal that is considered to be endangered, why is it endangered, and what is being done to help protect it?

2. **Research the topic.** See Information Sources.

3. **Plan the activity.**
   A. Materials
       information about one animal that is currently endangered
       pencils
       poster board or butcher paper
       colored felt pens, or paints and brushes

✱ Information Sources

Visit your library and find books about extinction and endangered species. One suggested book is *Evolution* by Linda Gamlin (New York: Dorling Kindersley Publishing, Inc., 1993). You can search the Internet by typing in these keywords: extinction and endangered species. Visit the United States Fish and Wildlife Service Web site for a list of threatened and endangered species of animals at ecos.fws.gov/tess_public/ TESSSpeciesReport. Also read the Background Information about threatened, endangered, and extinct animals on page 110 of this book.

B. Procedure

1. Read about the endangered animal you chose.

2. Create a large, colorful poster that tells people about the animal. Include the following: several drawings you have made of the animal; information about the animal and where it lives; why the animal has become endangered; and what is being done, if anything, to help protect it.

4. Do the activity. While you do the activity, keep notes on what you do, including things you observe and discover.

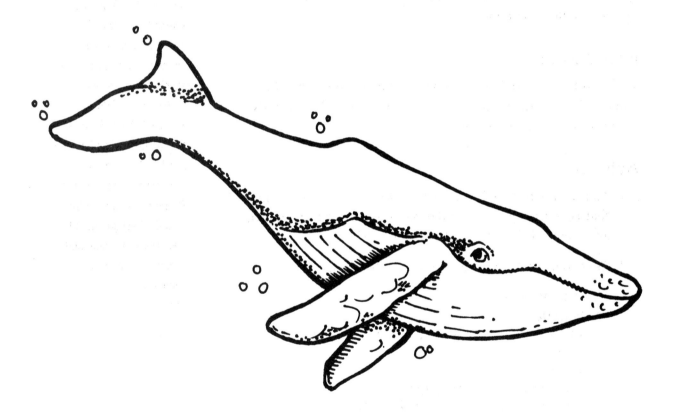

The humpback whale is an endangered species.

Background Information:
Threatened, Endangered, and Extinct Animals

An *extinct* animal is an animal that once lived on earth but no longer exists. Animals living in the wild that are close to becoming extinct are considered to be *endangered*. An animal that is close to becoming endangered is considered to be *threatened*. Plants can also become extinct, and they can also be considered endangered or threatened.

Extinction is a natural process that has always happened. Dinosaurs became extinct millions of years ago, probably because they couldn't adapt or adjust to a major change in the climate. But in the past several hundred years, thousands of plants and animals have become extinct because of things humans have done.

The greatest human cause of extinction is a loss of habitat. A habitat is the natural home where a particular animal lives. A loss of habitat can happen when people build houses, buildings, or roads through a plant's or animal's habitat. Another loss of habitat happens when trees that the animals live in or depend upon are cut down. An animal's body has become adapted to a particular habitat. Unlike people who can live in different locations, plants and animals usually cannot. If the habitat changes or is destroyed, the animal may not be able to adjust to the change. Sometimes it even becomes extinct.

Another cause of extinction is pollution. People have polluted lakes and rivers where animals live. Pesticides on farm crops can also destroy habitats for some animals, and so can air pollution.

A third cause of extinction is from over-hunting. People have killed animals for their body parts, including their fur, skin, teeth, horns, and feathers.

People called conservationists have been working to help protect endangered or threatened animals so they don't become extinct. Governments have also passed laws that help protect animals and their habitats.

Extension

Do research to learn about an endangered flower.

Category: Earth and Space Science
Topic: Plate Tectonics

Project 24:
Puzzling Plates

National Science Education Standards: Earth and Space Science, Content Standard D: Structure of the Earth System ("The solid earth is layered with a lithosphere; hot, convecting mantle; and a dense, metallic core" and "Lithospheric plates on the scales of continents and oceans constantly move at rates of centimeters per year in response to movements in the mantle.")

Introduction

With this project, you'll find out where Earth's major tectonic plates are located and in which direction they move.

Activity

1. **Ask a question.** Where are the tectonic plates located on earth?

2. **Research the topic.** See Information Sources.

3. **Plan the activity.**
   A. Materials
      three photocopies of the tectonic plate pattern (page 112), enlarged and printed on 11" x 17" paper
      three different colors of 11½" x 17" foam sheets (from craft store)
      straight pins
      sharp scissors
      glue
      ballpoint pen
      optional: thin magnetic strips that can be cut with scissors (from craft store)

Information Sources

Visit your library and find books about plate tectonics. Two suggested books are *How the Earth Works* by J. Farndon (New York: The Readers Digest Association, 1992) and *Time-Life Student Library: Planet Earth* (Virginia: Time-Life Books, 1997). You can search the Internet by typing in these keywords: plate tectonics and continental drift. Visit the Enchanted Learning Web site at www.enchantedlearning.com. Also read the Background Information about plate tectonics on page 115 of this book.

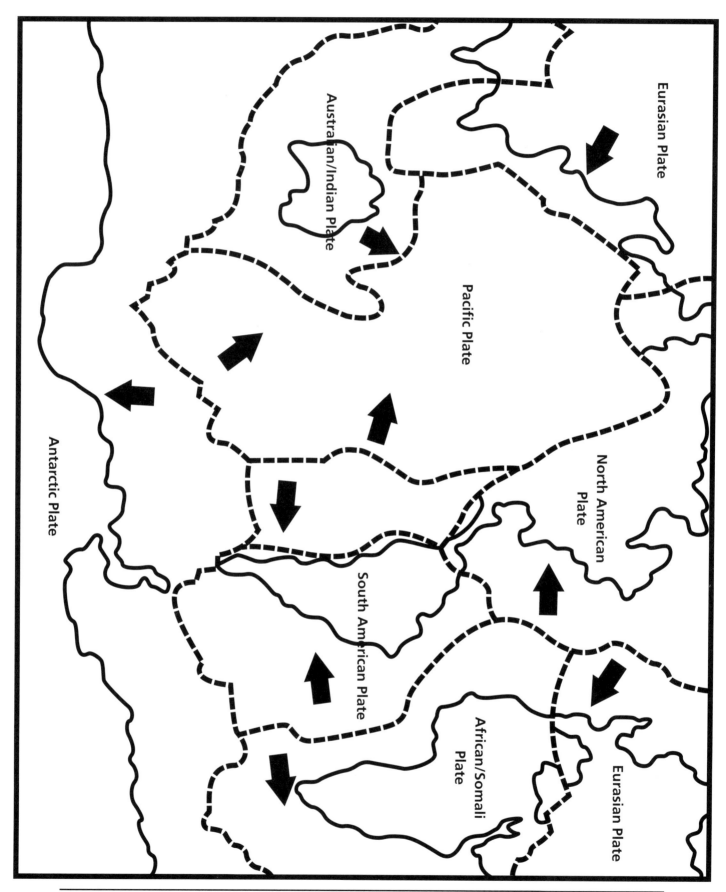

B. Procedure

1. First prepare the tectonic plates. To do this, take one of the photocopied plate patterns and cut off the excess paper beyond the heavy rectangular border and throw it away. Pin the pattern to one of the foam sheets. To help keep the pattern from wrinkling on the foam, try to keep the foam flat on the table as you pin. Also, start pinning at the top edge and work down the pattern to the bottom edge, smoothing out the pattern as you work. *Be careful of the sharp pins!* Cut around each heavy plate outline. Keep the foam as flat as possible on a table as you cut so the puzzle pieces don't wrinkle. After you cut out each plate, leave the pattern piece pinned to the plate.

2. Make the map of the tectonic plates. To do this, lay a second foam sheet on the table. This sheet will be a mat to set the puzzle on. Arrange the tectonic plate puzzle pieces from Step 1 on this mat where they belong. Keeping the puzzle together, carefully remove the pins and take off the paper pattern pieces.

3. Prepare the continents for the puzzle map. Cut the excess paper off another photocopied plate pattern. Pin this pattern on the third foam sheet. Cut around each continent. After you cut out each piece, unpin the paper pattern and place the foam puzzle piece where it goes on the puzzle map from Step 2. Use the third photocopied pattern as a guide. Glue the continent pieces in place on the plates. *Be sure you put glue on the back side of each continent.*

4. Label the puzzle map. Using the third photocopied pattern as a guide, label each plate with the pen. Also add the arrows, which show the general direction in which the plate drifts. Move the plates in the direction of their arrows. Which plates push together? Which pull apart? What is the name of the plate you live on and in what direction is it moving? The continents cover just some parts of the plates; what covers the rest of the plates?

5. Optional: Cut off pieces of magnetic strips and glue one piece to the back of each plate puzzle piece. Display your plate map on a refrigerator or other magnetic surface.

---

4. Do the activity. While you do the activity, keep notes on what you do, including things you observe and discover. On a table like the one shown below, record the names of the major plates. Note that the Eurasian Plate is shown in two places on the puzzle map; name it only once on the table. Also on the table, name any continents and oceans found on the plates—use an atlas to help you.

Name of Plate	Ocean(s) on plate	Continent(s) on plate
1.		
2.		
3.		
4.		
5.		
6.		
7.		

Background Information: Plate Tectonics

Our planet Earth is made up of different layers. The outermost layer is called the lithosphere. The lithosphere is broken into giant sections of solid rock called tectonic plates. These plates can contain continents, ocean floor, or both. Below the lithosphere is a layer called the athenosphere. Heat from inside the Earth keeps rock in the athenosphere so hot that it is like soft clay.

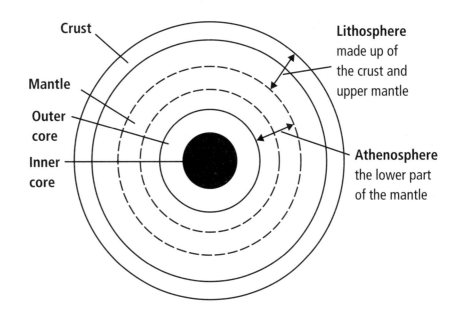

The heavy tectonic plates of the lithosphere can move. That's because they slide around on the softer athenosphere like your hand would slide around if it were pressed down on a mass of gooey peanut butter. But while you use energy to move your hand over the peanut butter, what energy causes the plates to move? Scientists believe that heat currents deep inside the athenosphere help pull the plates in different directions. These heat currents are called convection currents. Energy from the convection currents is strong enough to move the heavy plates about ½ inch (1.25 cm) each year! Sometimes the moving plates cause earthquakes.

The plates are locked tightly together around the surface of the Earth like floor tiles. When a plate moves, it bumps into the plates surrounding it. When two plates collide, their edges might wrinkle. Or the edge of one plate might curl below the edge of the other plate and melt in the hot mantle below. Plates can also spread apart. One place they do this is on the ocean floor. The gap between the spreading plates fills with melted rock that rises up from the mantle.

As the plates move, they cause the continents that ride on them to move. About 200 million years ago, all the continents were combined into one massive super continent called Pangaea. Over the years, the continents slowly drifted over the face of the Earth to their present positions. Where do you think the continents will be in the future?

Extension

In 1912, a German scientist named Alfred Wegener first proposed the idea that Earth was broken into plates and that they moved. Find out what other scientists thought of his idea at that time. What do scientists think of his ideas now?

Category: Earth and Space Science
Topic: Volcanoes

Project 25:
Three Erupting Volcanoes

National Science Education Standards: Earth and Space Science, Content Standard D: Structure of the Earth System ("Land forms are the result of a combination of constructive and destructive forces. Constructive forces include…volcanic eruptions.")

Introduction

With this project, you'll create three different types of volcanoes and watch them erupt.

Activity

1. **Ask a question.** What do the three types of volcanoes look like?

2. **Research the topic.** See Information Sources.

3. **Plan the activity.**
    A. Materials
        one cardboard paper towel tube
        scissors
        aluminum foil
        masking tape
        three sheets of heavy cardboard, 12 inches square
        one large mixing bowl
        1-cup measuring cup with a pouring spout
        8 cups of all-purpose flour
        2 cups salt
        3 cups water
        mixing spoon
        laundry marking pen
        paint brushes
        acrylic paints, non-toxic, in various earth-tone colors
            (from craft store)
        six clear 1-quart plastic bags
        two bricks (or boards about the same size as bricks)
        cider vinegar
        red tomato catsup
        baking soda

*** Information Sources**

Visit your library and find books about volcanoes. Three suggested books are *Volcanoes: Earth's Inner Fire* by Sally Walker (Minnesota: Carolrhoda Books, 1994), *Eyewitness: Volcano and Earthquake* by Susan Van Rose (New York: DK Publishing, Inc., 2004), and *The Best Book of Volcanoes* by Simon Adams (New York: Kingfisher, 2001). You can search the Internet by typing this keyword: volcanoes. Check out the United States Geological Survey Web site on volcanoes at pubs.usgs.gov/gip/volc and the Volcano World Web site at volcano.und.nodak.edu./vw.html. Also read the Background Information about volcanoes on pages 119–120 of this book.

B. Procedure

1. Prepare the vents for the volcanoes: To do this, cut the cardboard paper towel tube into three short tubes that are 1" long, 2" long, and 3" long. Cover the outsides of the three tubes with aluminum foil.

2. Prepare three pieces of "land" for each of the volcanoes. Have an adult cut a 1¼" diameter hole in the center of each sheet of cardboard. Cover the sheets of cardboard with foil. Punch a hole in the foil over the hole, push the cut foil edges down through the hole, and flatten them on the back of the cardboard. Center a short tube over the hole in each sheet of cardboard and tape the tubes in place.

3. Prepare the dough that will be used for all the volcanoes. In one large mixing bowl, place 8 cups of flour, 2 cups of salt, and 3 cups of water. Mix thoroughly with a spoon. When the dough becomes too thick to mix, continue mixing and squeezing the dough with your hands. Work the dough for about ten minutes until it is smooth and well-blended.

4. Build the three volcanoes. Use the illustration for the three types of volcanoes (page 120) to help you. Form the cinder cone around the 1" tube, the composite volcano around the 2" tube, and the shield volcano around the 3" tube. To make a volcano, place flattened balls of dough all around the tube and build them up into a volcano shape. Form each volcano into its proper shape and size. Leave approximately a 1-inch-diameter opening at the top of each volcano for the crater. Write the name of each volcano on the foil using the laundry marking pen.

5. Let the volcanoes dry for at least 3 days in a warm, dry area. Then, paint the volcanoes with the acrylic paint and let them dry for at least two more days.

---

6. Prepare the magma reservoirs for each volcano. Double up the quart-sized plastic bags to strengthen them by putting one bag inside the other. Push the bottom of one doubled plastic bag down through one of the volcano vents. Reach under the volcano, and pull the bag down through the hole in the cardboard. For the cinder cone and the shield volcano, the bottom of the bag should not hang down below the cardboard "land." For the composite cone, the bottom of the bag should hang down about two inches below the cardboard "land." Fold the top edges of the bags down over the top of each volcano to help protect it during the eruption.

7. Prepare the volcanoes for the eruptions. Take the three volcanoes outside. Set the cinder cone and shield volcano on the ground. Set the composite volcano on two bricks that are about five inches apart.

8. Have the cinder cone and the shield volcano erupt. To do this, pour ⅛ cup of baking soda into the cinder cone's magma reservoir. Pour the same amount of baking soda into the shield volcano. Add about ¼ cup of the vinegar to each volcano and watch them erupt. When vinegar and baking soda are mixed, they form bubbles of carbon dioxide gas. *Caution: Keep your face away from the top of the volcanoes while they are erupting!*

9. Have the composite volcano erupt. Pour ½ cup of baking soda into the composite volcano's magma reservoir. In a separate container, combine one cup vinegar with one tablespoon catsup and mix well. Reach one hand under the composite volcano and hold the magma reservoir bag. With the other hand, slowly pour the vinegar/catsup mixture into the magma reservoir. Slowly squeeze the magma reservoir bag to simulate pressure, creating a more violent eruption. *Caution: Keep your face away from the top of the volcano while it is erupting!*

4. Do the activity. While you do the activity, keep notes on what you do, including things you observe and discover. Record the information about the three volcanoes on a table like the one shown below.

Volcano type	Made of (check one)		Shape (draw it)	Size (check one)		
	Lava	Ash		Small	Med.	Large
Cinder Cone						
Shield						
Composite						

Background Information: Volcanoes

Volcanoes are mountains made of lava rock. The lava rock is formed deep inside the Earth where temperatures are over 1,000 degrees Fahrenheit (or 600 degrees Celsius)! This great heat can melt the rock into a liquid called magma. The magma floats up toward the surface of Earth and collects under the volcano in a chamber called a magma reservoir.

When the volcano erupts, magma starts flowing upward from the magma reservoir. It rises up through a vent to the peak of the volcano where there is often a bowl-shaped opening called a crater. The magma might also rise up through side vents along the slopes of the volcano.

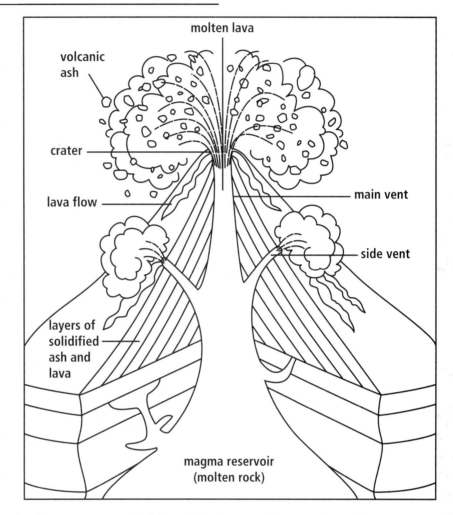

Once on the surface of Earth, the magma is called lava. The lava might ooze from the vents. Or built-up gases can shoot the lava out in a twirling display of fireworks. Gases can also cause hard bits of lava called volcanic ash to explode high into the air. Sometimes, steam from superheated water also billows out of the vents.

Volcanoes form in definite patterns around the world. An outer layer of Earth, called the lithosphere, is broken into giant sections of rock called plates. Most volcanoes occur at the boundaries of these plates.

There are three main types of volcanoes. The composite volcano is the most common type of volcano. It is formed from lava that is thick and slow-flowing. Composite volcanoes tend to have violent eruptions. That's because the thick lava traps gases, causing them to build up. Eventually, the gases explode, forcing volcanic ash out of the volcano and high into the air. Over time, the lava and ash build up in alternating layers to form a steep-sided volcano. Composite volcanoes are usually found where two of Earth's plates push together. Mount St. Helens in the state of Washington is a composite volcano.

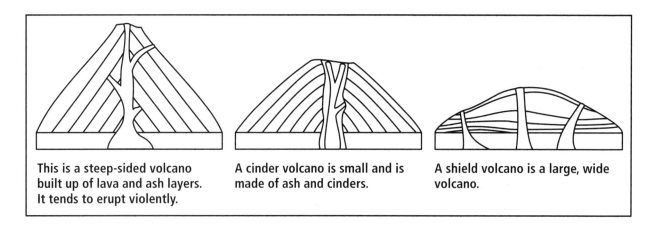

This is a steep-sided volcano built up of lava and ash layers. It tends to erupt violently.

A cinder volcano is small and is made of ash and cinders.

A shield volcano is a large, wide volcano.

The shield volcano is the largest volcano. It is formed from lava that is runny and fast-flowing. This type of lava oozes from the volcano and spreads out, creating a wide volcanic mountain with shallow sides. Many shield volcanoes are located over hot spots in the middle of Earth's plates. An example of a shield volcano is Kilauea in Hawaii.

The cinder cone is formed when volcanic ash and larger pieces called cinders pile up in a mound. These are the smallest volcanoes. They are usually found near larger volcanoes.

Extension

Find out where volcanoes tend to occur around the world. Also find about the "Ring of Fire" and why so many volcanoes occur in this area.

Category: **Earth and Space Science**
Topic: **Rock Cycle**

Project 26:
Recycled Rocks

National Science Education Standards: Earth and Space Science, Content Standard D: Structure of the Earth System ("Land forms are the result of a combination of constructive and destructive forces. Constructive forces include crustal deformation…and deposition of sediment. Destructive forces include weathering and erosion.")

Introduction

With this project, you will learn about the rock cycle and the three types of rocks.

Activity

1. **Ask a question.** What is the rock cycle, and how does it work?

2. **Research the topic.** See Information Sources.

3. **Plan the activity.**
   A. Materials
   9" x 10" sheet of white construction paper
   9" x 10" sheet of corrugated cardboard
     (use part of a cardboard box)
   pencil
   colored pencils or crayons
   brushes
   two 3" x 4" rectangles of heavy cardboard
   scissors
   rock samples of each of the three different types of rocks
   masking tape
   pen
   rock identification book (available in libraries and bookstores)

* Information Sources

Visit your library and find books about rocks and the rock cycle. Two suggested books are *Eyewitness: Rocks and Minerals* by Dr. R.F. Symes (New York: DK Publishing, Inc., 2004) and *National Audubon Society First Field Book of Rocks and Minerals* by Edward Ricciuti and Margaret W. Carruthers (New York: Scholastic, Inc., 1998). You can search the Internet by typing in these keywords: rocks and the rock cycle. Also read the Background Information about the rock cycle on pages 123–124 of this book.

B. Procedure

1. Make a large rock cycle illustration. To do this, use the pencil to sketch an illustration of the rock cycle on the white sheet of construction paper. Use the illustration of the rock cycle (page 123) to help you. Color your illustration with colored pencils or crayons. Glue your illustration to the sheet of cardboard.

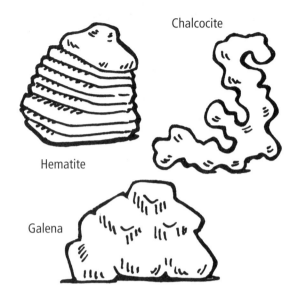

Chalcocite

Hematite

Galena

3. Make a stand for your rock cycle illustration so it can sit upright. Take the two 3" x 4" rectangles of cardboard. Snip a slot that's 1½" deep in the middle of one of the longer sides of each of the rectangles. Along the bottom edge of the cardboard on your rock cycle illustration, snip two 1½" deep slots. These slots should be about 8" apart. Slip the smaller pieces of cardboard into the slits you made on the illustration.

4. Collect different kinds of rocks. Use a rock identification book to help you name the rocks and their types—igneous, sedimentary, or metamorphic. If you're able to identify a rock, write its name and type on a small piece of masking tape. Stick the masking tape on the rock. If you're unsure of the rock's name, try to at least figure out its type. Group the rocks together by type and set them out around your rock cycle illustration. If you can't find actual rocks, try drawing some of the different kinds of rocks you see in the rock identification book.

4. Do the activity. While you do the activity, keep notes on what you do, including things you observe and discover. If you found actual rock samples, record the names and types of rocks you found on a table like the one shown below.

Name of rock	Type of rock (check one)		
	Igneous	Sedimentary	Metamorphic
1.			
2.			
3.			
4.			
5.			
6.			

Background Information: The Rock Cycle

The rock cycle is the continuous circulation of rocks through Earth's crust and on the surface. As rocks move through the cycle, they can change form.

The cycle begins with igneous rock. Igneous rock is formed when hot magma deep inside the earth rises up toward the surface and cools and hardens. If the magma stays inside the crust, it is called intrusive igneous rock. But the magma can also erupt onto the surface through a volcano. Once magma reaches the surface, it is called lava. Lava hardens on the surface into a rock called extrusive igneous rock.

Extrusive igneous rock on the surface of Earth can change into sedimentary rock. First, the rock is slowly broken down into smaller pieces by sunlight, wind, rain, ice, and snow. This process is called weathering. These pieces of rock are eventually carried by wind, rain, and rivers to the ocean. Layers of rock build up on the ocean floor. Over time, they can press together to form sedimentary rock.

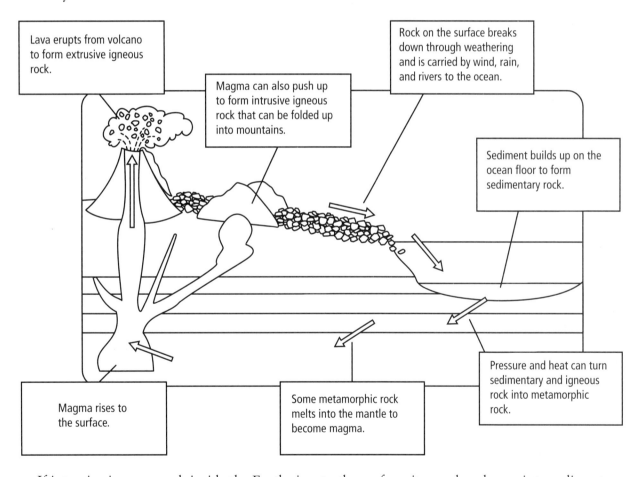

Lava erupts from volcano to form extrusive igneous rock.

Magma can also push up to form intrusive igneous rock that can be folded up into mountains.

Rock on the surface breaks down through weathering and is carried by wind, rain, and rivers to the ocean.

Sediment builds up on the ocean floor to form sedimentary rock.

Magma rises to the surface.

Some metamorphic rock melts into the mantle to become magma.

Pressure and heat can turn sedimentary and igneous rock into metamorphic rock.

If intrusive igneous rock inside the Earth rises to the surface, it can also change into sedimentary rock. Some mountains have intrusive igneous rock inside them. As the mountain erodes or wears away over time, the rock inside becomes exposed. This intrusive igneous rock can then break down and end up on the ocean floor. There it can form into sedimentary rock.

Both igneous rock and sedimentary rock can also change into metamorphic rock. Earth's crust is broken into huge sections called plates. As the plates move around, igneous rock and sedimentary rock are carried down into the crust. Great heat and pressure there can change the rocks into metamorphic rock.

If any of the types of rock—igneous, sedimentary, or metamorphic—are heated enough while inside the Earth, they can melt into magma. The magma can then rise toward the surface to become either intrusive or extrusive igneous rock. And so the rock cycle continues.

Extension

Consider making rock collecting your hobby. You can store your rocks in an empty egg carton.

Earth and Space Science
Topic: Weather: Wind

Project 27:
Wind Watching

National Science Education Standards: Earth and Space Science, Content Standard D: Structure of the Earth System ("Global patterns of atmospheric movement influence local weather.")

Introduction

With this project, you will observe the wind and make two kinds of instruments that measure it.

Activity

1. **Ask a question.** How do the direction and speed of the wind relate to the type of weather we'll have where I live?

2. **Research the topic.** See Information Sources.

3. **Plan the activity.**
   A. Materials
   Wind direction finder—
      ribbon, one inch wide by one foot long (or a piece of lightweight fabric cut to that size)
      scissors
      paper clip
      laundry marker
      pencil (unsharpened, with eraser)
      one photocopy of the wind direction pattern (page 126), enlarged so that the outer circle is about 4" in diameter
      tape
      magnetic compass

   Anemometer—
      one photocopy of the anemometer pattern (page 126)
      manila file folder
      glue
      scissors
      hole punch
      brass paper fastener
      thread, 1 foot long
      plastic table tennis (ping-pong) ball
      tape
      ruler

* Information Sources
Visit your library and find books about the wind. Two suggested books are *Eyewitness: Weather* by Brian Cosgrove (New York: DK Publishing, Inc., 2004) and *How the Weather Works* by Michael Allaby (New York: The Reader's Digest Association, Inc., 1995.) You can search the Internet by typing in these keywords: wind and weather. Also read the Background Information about wind on page 129 of this book.

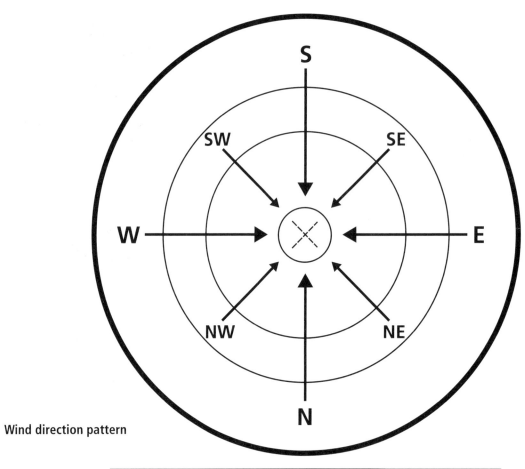

Wind direction pattern

Anemometer

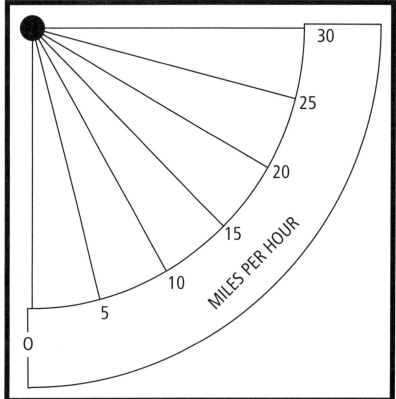

B. Procedure

Wind direction finder—

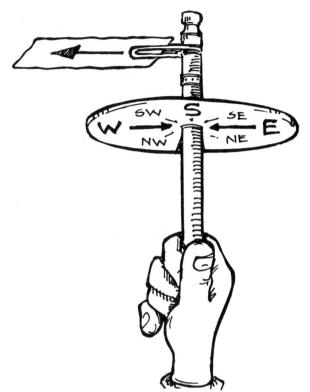

1. Use the scissors to snip a tiny hole in one end of the ribbon. Poke the end of the paper clip through the hole and twist the paper clip around until it is hooked into the ribbon. With the laundry marker, draw a short arrow on the ribbon near the paper clip. The arrow should point *away* from the paper clip.

2. Push the push pin into middle of the paper clip that is attached to the ribbon. Push the push pin part way into the top of the pencil eraser. The ribbon and paper clip should spin freely around the push pin.

3. Cut out the wind direction pattern. Snip an "X" shape in the center of the pattern. Slide the pencil down through the "X." The pattern should be about halfway up the pencil. The printed side of the wind direction pattern should face *downward* toward the unsharpened end of the pencil. Tape the top side of the pattern to the pencil.

4. To use the wind direction finder, go outside to an open area on a windy day. Use the magnetic compass to find north. Then hold up the pencil above your head so that the "N" on the wind direction pattern faces north. Look at the ribbon and see what direction the arrow you drew on it is pointing. Then look to see which arrow on the wind direction pattern on the opposite side of the pencil is parallel to it *and* also pointing in the same direction. The wind direction finder shows from what direction the wind is blowing. If the matching arrow on the wind direction finder is marked "N," then the wind is blowing from the north.

Anemometer—

1. Cut around the anemometer pattern and discard the excess paper. Set the pattern on the file folder, with the top edge of the pattern along the fold of the file folder. Glue the pattern in place. Then cut around the pattern so you have two layers of the file folder. Throw away the excess file folder.

2. Use the hole punch to make a hole in the small black circle on the anemometer and through the file folder. Poke a paper fastener into the hole. Leave a tiny gap behind the round head of the paper fastener so it isn't tight against the anemometer. Fold out the flaps of the paper fastener against the back of the anemometer.

---

3. Tie one end of the thread around the paper fastener. Tape the other end of the thread to the ball. Hold up the anemometer so its bottom edge is parallel to the ground. Make sure the thread hangs vertically and is directly in front of the zero line on the anemometer. If it doesn't hang vertically, move the paper fastener in the hole until it does. Once the thread is lined up correctly, tape the flaps of the paper fastener on the back of the anemometer in place.

4. Tape the left edge (the side with the string) and bottom edge closed, being careful not to catch the string on the left side in the tape. Slip a ruler into the open right side so the ruler is horizontal and parallel to the top edge. The ruler will act as a handle for the anemometer.

5. To measure the wind speed, first find the direction the wind is blowing by using your wind direction finder. Face that direction and hold the ruler "handle" on your anemometer out in front of you so it is parallel to the ground. The zero on the scale should be away from you. If there's wind, it will blow the ball toward you. Read the number on the anemometer where the thread crosses the scale. This number shows the wind speed in miles per hour.

4. **Do the activity.** While you do the activity, keep notes on what you do, including things you observe and discover. Make observations on seven different days. Record the results of your wind measurements on a table like the one shown below. Also record the current weather. Is it sunny or cloudy? Warm or cold? Calm or windy? Dry or stormy? Is there a pattern between wind direction, wind speed, and the type of weather that happens?

	Date	Wind direction	Wind speed	Current weather
1.				
2.				
3.				
4.				
5.				
6.				
7.				

Background Information: Wind

Wind is air that is moving. Wind mainly happens because the sun heats the surface of the Earth unevenly. When an area on the surface is heated, it warms the air just above it. This warmed mass of air expands and becomes light enough to float upward into the atmosphere. This rising mass of warm air creates an area of low pressure near the ground.

At the same time, cooler, heavier air nearby sinks toward the ground, creating an area of high pressure The colder air flows in to replace the rising, warm air. That's because air moves from areas of high pressure to low pressure. This circulation of air from high pressure to low pressure is called a convection current. Wind is the moving air in a convection current.

Wind speed is a measure of how fast the wind is blowing. The greater the difference between the high pressure area the low pressure area, the greater the wind speed. Wind speed is measured with an instrument called an anemometer. There are many different kinds of anemometers.

Wind direction is the direction from which the wind is blowing. A north wind blows from the north and a southeast wind blows from the southeast. Wind direction is measured with wind vanes, wind socks, and also flags on vertical poles.

Wind can carry weather from one location to another. It can move hot or cold air, dry or moist air, and even clouds and storms.

There is often a link between wind direction and speed and the type of weather the wind tends to bring to a certain area.

Extension

Find out about other kinds of instruments that measure wind direction and wind speed. Also find out about the Beaufort Wind Scale.

Category: Earth and Space Science
Topic: History of Earth

Project 28:
Geologic Time Scale

National Science Education Standards: Earth and Space Science, Content Standard D: Earth's History ("The earth processes we see today, including erosion, movement of lithospheric plates, and changes in atmospheric composition, are similar to those that occurred in the past. Earth history is also influenced by occasional catastrophes, such as the impact of an asteroid or comet." "Fossils provide important evidence of how life and environmental conditions have changed.")

Introduction

With this project, you'll make a geologic time scale that shows the history of the Earth starting billions of years ago. You'll also get to ask people some questions about Earth's long history to see what they know.

Activity

1. **Ask a question.** What is the geologic history of the Earth?

2. **Research the topic.** See Information Sources.

3. **Plan the activity.**
   A. Materials
       11 sheets of 9" x 12" construction paper: 5 sheets of red, 3 sheets of orange, 2 sheets of yellow, and 1 sheet of green
       scissors
       clear packaging tape (or regular clear tape)
       optional: laundry marking pen
       yardstick (or meter stick)
       pencils, crayons

> ***Information Sources***
>
> Visit your library and find books about the geologic time scale. Two suggested books are *How the Earth Works* by J. Farndon (New York: The Readers Digest Association, 1992) and *Eyewitness: Future* by Michael Tambini (New York: DK Publishing, Inc., 2004). You can search the Internet by typing in this keyword: geologic time scale. Visit the Enchanted Learning Web site at www.enchantedlearning.com. Also read the Background Information about the geologic time scale on page 133 of this book.

B. Procedure

1. Cut each sheet of paper in half, widthwise. You will not need the other half of the green sheet.

2. Lay the half-sheets in one long line on the floor. They should be in this order from left to right: ten red, six orange, four yellow, and one green. The longer sides of the sheets should be next to each other but not quite touching.

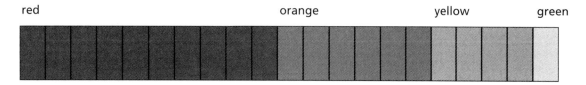

3. Run tape down the edges between two neighboring sheets of paper. Be sure to leave a tiny gap between the pages when you tape. This gap will make it easier to later fold up the pages into a booklet. Each page represents about 50 million years. The single green page represents the 65 million years of the Cenozoic Era. The four yellow pages represent the almost 200 million years of the Mesozoic Era. The six orange pages represent the almost 300 million years of the Paleozoic Era. The ten red pages represent the 4 billion years of the Precambrian Era. Notice there are not enough pages to represent all 4 billion years of the Precambrian Era; if there were, there would be about 80 pages! So for this era, the first 250 million years and the last 250 million years will be represented by the ten pages. Optional: If you wish, you can show that a period of time is missing for part of the red pages. To do this use the laundry marker to draw two parallel zig-zagged lines between the fifth and sixth sheets of red paper.

4. Flip your geologic time scale over so the taped side is facing down. The single green page should still be to the right. Use the yardstick to draw one long, continuous line across all the pages that are taped together. The line should be about three inches down from the top of the pages.

5. Use the geologic time scale table on page 134 to help you with this step. In the spaces *above* the long line you drew in Step 4, write the names of the four eras. Leave room just above and below the era names, and center each era name in the middle of the colored sheets for that era. Below the four era names and just above the long line, write in the "years ago" numbers for each era. These numbers should be written on the vertical dividing lines between two different colored era sheets. You can write "MYA" to stand for a "million years ago." Above the era names, write the two eon names. Write "Precambrian Era" in the middle of the red sheets. Write "Phanerozoic Era" in the center of the remaining sheets.

6. In the spaces *below* the long line you drew in Step 4, write in what happened during each era. You can also draw pictures. You might list the physical features of the Earth in one section of the space and organisms, like plants and animals, in another space. Use the geologic time scale table on page 134 to help you with this step.

7. Carefully fold the entire time scale back along the long line across all the pages. Gently run the side of a pencil down this long fold to make a sharp crease. Turn the geologic time scale so you only see the upper side with the eons, eras, and "years ago" numbers you wrote.

8. Show only the upper side of your time scale to at least five different people. Have them guess during which era different events happened, such as when they think the Earth was first formed, when dinosaurs first appeared, or when the continents were all bunched together into one mass. When you are done questioning each person, unfold the table so the person can see which answers they got right.

9. Store your geologic time scale like a book by unfolding it along the long line so all the sheets are flat, and then folding it up accordion style along the taped edges.

4. Do the activity. While you do the activity, keep notes on what you do, including things you observe and discover. Use a table like the one shown below to record the questions you asked each person in Step 8 and their answers.

Geologic Time Scale Questionnaire

Respondent: _____   **Date:** _____

Question	Responses (check one)			
	Precambrian	**Paleozoic**	**Mesozoic**	**Cenozoic**
1. During what era do you think dinosaurs first appeared on earth?				
2.				
3.				
4.				
5.				

Background Information: Geologic Time Scale

The geologic time scale is a table showing the history of Earth's physical features and life forms. It begins 4,600,000,000 (4.6 billion) years ago, when scientists believe Earth was formed. The time scale continues to the present time.

Scientists did many studies to figure out the time scale. They studied fossils to find out what kinds of life once lived on Earth. A fossil is the remains or traces of a plant or animal from long ago. To find the approximate age of the fossils, scientists studied how far down in the ground the fossils were buried. Rock and dirt usually build up from bottom to top, so the oldest layers are on the bottom. That means the oldest fossils are also in the bottom layers. Scientists also use a process called radioactive dating to find the ages of once-living things.

From their studies, scientists noticed that during a number of times over the years, animals and life forms have become extinct or have died out. Scientists are not exactly sure why, but some causes might be from major volcanic eruptions, major changes in Earth's climate, and asteroids from space hitting our planet.

The geologic time scale is divided into two main periods of time called eons. The eons are further broken down into four eras. Scientists know least about the Precambrian Era because it was so long ago that there are few clues left behind to study. The eras are also broken down into much smaller periods of time. Note: "Paleo-" means ancient, "meso-" means middle, and "ceno-'" means recent.

Extension

What do you think the future will be like during the next era on the geologic time scale? What will the era be called? What kinds of land forms will be created or break up? What kinds of plants and animals will there be? What will humans be like?

Name: _____

GEOLOGIC TIME SCALE
(not to scale)

	PRECAMBRIAN	PHANEROZOIC		
Eon	PRECAMBRIAN	PHANEROZOIC		
Era	Hadean–Archaean–Proterozoic 4 billion years	Paleozoic 296 million years	Mesozoic 183 million years	Cenozoic 65 million years
Million Years Ago (MYA)	4,500	544	248	65 0
Physical Features of Earth	Earth first forms as a fiery hot rock that slowly cools. Many volcanoes erupt. Gasses combine to form first atmosphere with oxygen. Rain fills oceans. Earth's surface breaks into large chunks called plates, which slowly move.	Earth's moving plates bunch together to form one supercontinent called Pangaea. Warm, shallow seas cover most of North America and then later recede. Appalachian mountains form. Coal-forming forests thrive. Some desert regions appear.	Pangaea starts breaking up. Atlantic Ocean begins forming. Mountain building starts in western North America and the Rocky Mountains form.	Continents move to present-day locations. Alps, Himalaya, and Sierra Nevada mountains form. Grand Canyon forms.
Living things	Single-cell organisms such as algae appear. Later, many-celled animals like worms and jelly-fish appear.	Animals without backbones such as trilobites appear. Later, insects, fish, amphibians, and reptiles appear. Marine plants and later land plants appear. Toward end of era, many animals without backbones become extinct.	Mammals and birds appear. Dinosaurs flourish and later become extinct. Flowering plants and conifers appear.	Many mammals appear. Modern humans (Homo sapiens) appear.

Category: Earth and Space Science
Topic: Solar System

Project 29:
Our Solar System

National Science Education Standards: Earth and Space Science, Content Standard D: Earth in the Solar System ("The earth is the third planet from the sun in a system that includes the moon, the sun, nine planets and their moons, and smaller objects, such as asteroids and comets." "The sun, an average star, is the central and largest body in the solar system." "Most objects in the solar system are in regular and predictable motion.")

Introduction

With this project, you'll explore our solar system to find out about the sun and the planets spinning around it.

Activity

1. **Ask a question.** What objects make up our solar system, and where are they located?

2. **Research the topic.** See Information Sources

3. **Plan the activity.**
   A. **Materials**
      two 2" x 45" (5 cm x 114 cm) strips of heavy cardboard
      ruler (with centimeters)
      pencil
      manila file folders
      drawing compass for making circles
      glue
      colored pencils or crayons
      sewing needle
      thread
      tape
      Hula Hoop
      white butcher paper
      optional: paint

> *** Information Sources**
>
> Visit your library and find books about our solar system. Two suggested books are *Eyewitness: Astronomy* by Kristen Lippincott (New York: DK Publishing, 2004) and *How the Universe Works* by Heather Couper and Nigel Henbest (New York: Reader's Digest Young Families, Inc., 1994). You can search the Internet by typing in these keywords: solar system and planets. Also read the Background Information about our solar system on page 139 of this book.

B. Procedure

1. Locate where the sun will be on the model. To do this, lay one of the cardboard strips out in front of you, with one of its long sides toward you. Use the ruler to measure ten centimeters from the left (shorter) edge of the strip. Draw a mark at this location and label it "sun." This is where the outer edge of the sun will go.

2. Locate the distance from the sun to each of the plants on the cardboard strip from Step 1. To do this, start at the sun mark you made in step 1 (*not the edge of the cardboard*) and measure the distances to each planet. Make a mark for each of the distances, and write the name of the planet next to each mark. Use the distances shown on the table below. Note: The distances from the sun have been scaled down so that 150,000,000 km (the distance from sun to the Earth) is represented by 2.5 centimeters.

Object	Distance from sun (scale: 150,000,000 km = 2.5 cm; figures rounded)	Radius of object (scale: 12,756 km = 1 cm; figures rounded)	Radius of rings of gaseous giants (not to scale)		Suggested color
			Inner edge	Outer edge	
Sun	——	55 cm	——	——	yellow & orange
Mercury	1.00 cm	.20 cm	——	——	silver
Venus	1.80 cm	.35 cm	——	——	yellow
Earth	2.50 cm	.50 cm	——	——	blue & green
Mars	3.80 cm	.25 cm	——	——	red
Jupiter	13.00 cm	5.50 cm	4.5 cm	7.5 cm	light yellow
Saturn	24.00 cm	5.00 cm	4.0 cm	7.0 cm	yellow stripes
Uranus	48.00 cm	2.00 cm	1.0 cm	3.0 cm	blue-green
Neptune	75.00 cm	2.00 cm	1.0 cm	3.0 cm	blue
Pluto	99.00 cm	0.10 cm	——	——	dark blue

3. Make the planets for the model. The planets will be represented by flat disks cut from the manila file folders. To draw a circle for a planet, first lay the ruler on a file folder. Push the point of the compass into the file folder at the zero mark on the ruler. Open out the compass and set the point of the pencil next to the correct centimeter mark on the ruler for that planet. For the centimeter mark, use the *radius* figures shown on the table above. A radius is half the diameter of a circle. Make sure there is plenty of manila folder paper around the zero mark so you can draw a full circle. Then draw the circle with the compass. Cut out the planet and lightly write the name of the planet on it. Note: The radius figures have been scaled down so that 6,380 km (the approximate radius of Earth) equals 0.5 centimeter.

4. Make a ring for each of the four gaseous giants. To make the rings, first draw a smaller circle on a file folder to represent the inner edge of the ring around the planet. Leave the metal point of the compass in this same position on the folder. Then open up the compass and draw the outer edge of the ring. Use the inner and outer ring radius figures shown on the table above. Cut out the ring and lightly label it with the name of the planet. Note: The rings are simply used to show which of the planets have them; they are not to any scale on this model.

5. Color the planets and rings. Saturn has the most rings, so you might color its ring with many stripes.

6. Attach the rings to the gaseous giant planets. To do this, lay one edge of the ruler across the diameter of one of the gaseous giants. At both ends of the diameter marking, cut a short slit that's about a centimeter long. Slip the planet's ring down over the planet and fit it into the slits to hold it in place. The ring should be perpendicular to the flat planet disk.

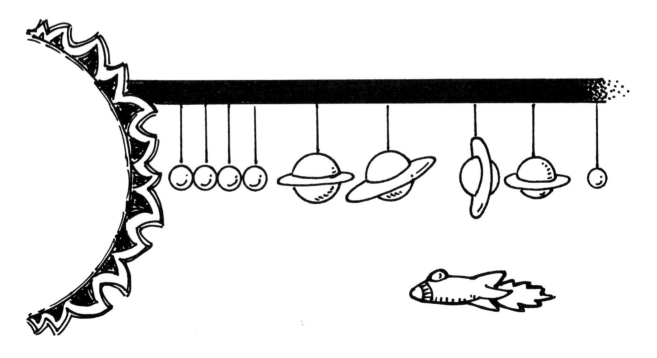

7. Attach the planets to the cardboard strip. To do this, thread the sewing needle. Poke the needle through the top of a planet, and pull the needle through until about a foot of loose thread hangs out on either side of the planet. Cut the thread. Repeat for each planet. Note: The rings of Saturn are slightly slanted, so poke the needle through the planet near one edge of the ring. Lay the cardboard strip flat on a table. Set out the planets under the cardboard strip in a line in order from left to right. Tape the tops of the threads for each planet to the marking for that planet on the cardboard strip.

8. Glue the second cardboard strip to the cardboard strip with the planets hanging on it from Step 7. The taped strings attached to the planets should be sandwiched in between the two strips. Optional: You can paint the outer sides of the cardboard strips black or another color of your choice.

9. Make part of the sun and attach it to the second cardboard strip. To do this, set part of the Hula Hoop on the butcher paper so the hoop overlaps the edge of the paper by about seven centimeters. Trace around the Hula Hoop on the paper to make part of a circle. Then draw jagged lines around the circle you drew to represent sun rays. The points of the sun rays should not extend more than three centimeters beyond the circle you drew. Cut out the sun, and trace it onto another piece of butcher paper so you have two identical pieces. Glue the two sun pieces together to make one thick sun. Color the sun. Tape the top of the sun to one end of the second cardboard strip. The flat edge of the sun should be lined up with the short edge of the strip. Note: The actual radii (radii is plural for radius) of the planets in our solar system are tiny compared to the distances the planets are from the sun. So for this model, the scale used for the planet radii is *not* the same as the scale used for the distances. If they did match, either the radius sizes of the planets would be too tiny, or the distances from the sun would be too great to use on a model like this.

4. Do the activity. While you do the activity, keep notes on what you do, including things you observe and discover. Create your own table that has some basic information about the sun and the planets, such as distances, radius sizes, and colors. Use the information from your research. You can also use information from the table of sun and planets shown on page 139.

Background Information: Our Solar System

Our solar system is made up of the sun, along with nine planets and other smaller objects which travel around it. Solar means sun. Our solar system is part of the Milky Way galaxy. A galaxy is a grouping of millions of stars.

Scientists believe the solar system formed about 4,600,000,000 (4.6 billion) years ago. They aren't sure exactly how it formed, but one idea is that it started with a slowly-rotating cloud made of dust and gases. Later, some of the cloud material pulled inward to form a large central mass, which is the sun. Outer cloud material continued moving around the sun and pieces of it clumped together to become the nine planets.

Since then, the planets have continued to revolve around the sun. The force of gravity between the sun and the planets keeps them in place. Each of the planets also spins or rotates on its own axis.

The sun is a star made up mostly of hydrogen and helium gases. It is considered to be an average-sized star. But it is so huge that its diameter is 110 times greater than Earth's!

The four planets nearest the sun, called the terrestrial (Earth-like) planets, are small and made up of rock. The terrestrial planets are Mercury, Venus, Earth, and Mars.

The next four planets are large and made up mostly of gases, so they are referred to as the gaseous giants. The gaseous giants are Jupiter, Saturn, Uranus, and Neptune. These planets have particles of dust and rock encircling them, which form rings around the planets. Saturn has the most rings. Uranus spins sideways on its axis, so its rings spin almost vertically around it like a wheel.

Pluto is the last planet. It is neither a terrestrial planet nor a gaseous giant. Pluto is small and believed to be made up of both rock and ice.

Object	Composition	Diameter (km)	Average distance to sun (km)	Rotation time (hours)	Number of moons	Number of rings
Sun	gases	1,400,000	—	—	—	—
Mercury	rock	4,878	58,000,000	4,224		0
Venus	rock	12,104	108,000,000	2,808		0
Earth	rock	12,756	150,000,000	24	1	0
Mars	rock	6,974	228,000,000	24	2	0
Jupiter	gases	142,796	778,000,000	10	16	1
Saturn	gases	120,660	1,427,000,000	10	18	many
Uranus	gases	51,118	2,870,000,000	17	15	11
Neptune	gases	49,528	4,497,000,000	16	8	4
Pluto	rock, ice, gases	2,290	5,900,000,000	153	1	0

Extension

Other objects in our solar system are comets, asteroids, and meteoroids. Do research to learn about them.

Category: Earth and Space Science
Topic: The Moon

Project 30:
Moon Tracker

National Science Education Standards: Earth and Space Science, Content Standard D: Earth in the Solar System ("The earth is the third planet from the sun in a system that includes the moon…" "Most objects in the solar system are in regular and predictable motion. Those motions explain such phenomena as…the phases of the moon, and the eclipses.")

Introduction

With this project, you'll find out what causes the phases of the moon and also keep track of what the moon's glow looks like over a month.

Activity

1. **Ask a question.** What causes the moon's different phases over a month, and what do the phases look like?

2. **Research the topic.** See Information Sources.

3. **Plan the activity.**
   A. Materials
   Moon dial—
      one photocopy of the moon dial pattern (page 141), enlarged and printed on 8½" by 11" paper
      scissors
      glue
      manila file folder (or other lightweight cardboard such as from a cold cereal box)
      hole punch
      1 brass paper fastener (brad)

   Moon calendar—
      one photocopy of monthly calendar pages that cover the next thirty days
      pencil
      a small lid (about ¾" in diameter) or other small round object to trace
      clipboard (a piece of stiff cardboard and 2 clothespins also work well)
      pencil
      colored pencils
      watch

> *** Information Sources**
> Visit your library and find books about the moon. One suggested book is *The Best Book of the Moon* by Ian Graham (New York: King-fisher: 1999). You can search the Internet by typing in these keywords: moon and moon phases. The Almanac web page shows the phases of the moon for specific months: www.almanac.com/astronomy/moon/index.php. Also read the Background Information about the moon on pages 143–144 of this book.

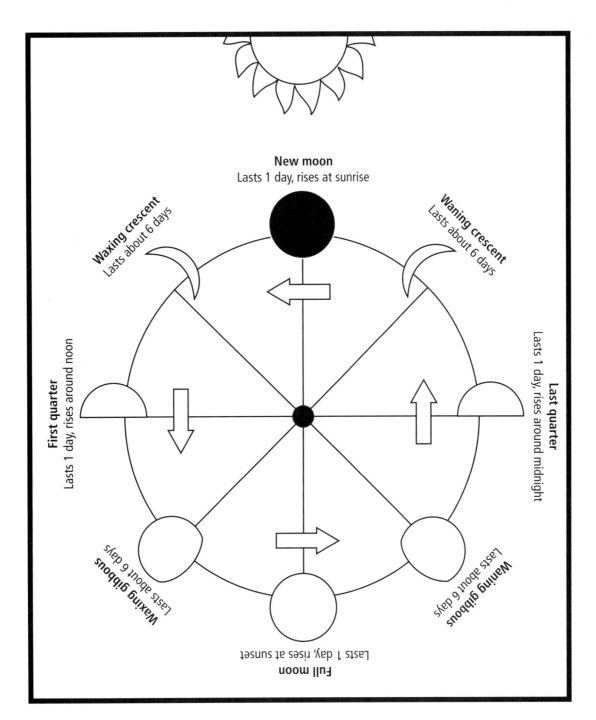

New moon
Lasts 1 day, rises at sunrise

Waxing crescent
Lasts about 6 days

Waning crescent
Lasts about 6 days

First quarter
Lasts 1 day, rises around noon

Last quarter
Lasts 1 day, rises around midnight

Waxing gibbous
Lasts about 6 days

Waning gibbous
Lasts about 6 days

Full moon
Lasts 1 day, rises at sunset

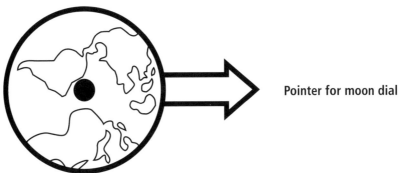

Pointer for moon dial

B. Procedure

Moon dial—

1. Cut out the photocopied moon dial pattern and the pointer. Glue each piece to the file folder. Cut around each shape again and throw away the excess cardboard.

2. Use the hole punch to make a hole in the small black circle in the middle of the moon dial. Make another hole in the small black circle on the pointer. Set the pointer on the moon dial, and line up the holes. Poke a paper fastener through both holes. Fold out the back flaps of the paper fastener against the back of the moon dial.

3. To use the moon dial, hold it and move the pointer so it points to one of the moon phases on the dial. Leaving the pointer in this position, turn the moon dial itself around so the pointer you set points away from you. This is how that phase would look to you from Earth. To see how each phase looks from Earth, continue moving the pointer around the dial in a counterclockwise direction. Notice that the sun illustration is at one edge of the moon dial and that the glowing side of the moon always faces that direction.

Moon calendar—

1. Clip the photocopied calendar pages to the clipboard. Use the small lid to trace a circle on each date box of the calendar. You will be filling in these circles with the shape of the moon glow. Each day for the next thirty days, observe the moon and draw a picture of the shape of its glow in the circles on your calendar. Below the picture, write the time that you observed the moon. For this project, you don't have to look at the moon at the same time each day. If you can't see the moon on a specific day, leave the square blank.

2. Keep your moon dial with your moon tracker. As the actual moon changes to the next main phase, move the pointer on the moon dial counterclockwise so it points to the current moon phase.

4. **Do the activity.** While you do the activity, keep notes on what you do, including things you observe and discover.

Background Information: The Moon

The moon is Earth's natural satellite. Satellites are objects that travel around other objects. It takes the moon almost a month to travel all the way around the Earth. While the moon is moving around the Earth, the Earth is busy making its year-long trip around the sun.

From Earth, we can see the moon glowing in the sky. But the moon itself doesn't make the light. The moon glows because the sun shines on it, just like an object such as a wall lights up when you shine a flashlight on it.

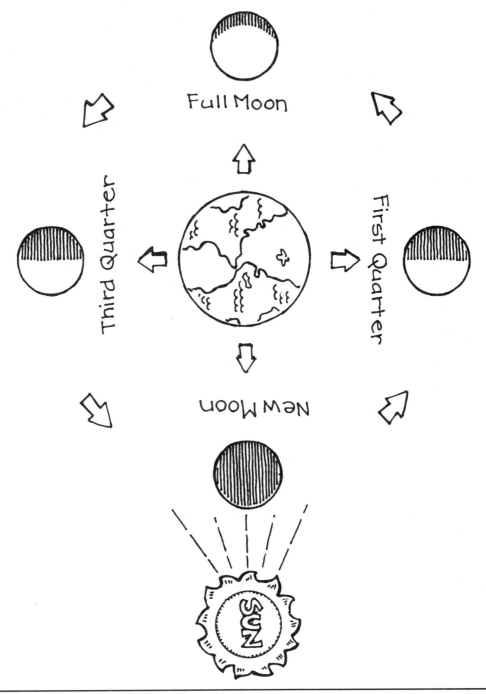

The shape of the moon's glow appears to change as it moves around the Earth. That's because each day of its month-long trip around Earth, the moon is in a slightly different position in the sky. These different positions mean we see the sunlight hitting the moon from slightly different angles.

Each different shape of the moon's glow is called a phase. During the new moon phase, the sun is behind the moon, so you usually can't see the moon. For the next six days, the moon is in the waxing crescent phase. Waxing means it is getting bigger. There's a thin glow on the right side of the moon that grows larger each day. The glow is on the right because the sun is shining on it from that direction.

When the glow becomes large enough to cover the right half of the moon, the sun is in the first quarter phase for about a day. For the six following days, the moon is in the waxing gibbous phase. During this phase, the moon's glow covers over half the right side of the moon, and the glow continues to grow larger.

When the moon is a completely glowing circle, it is in the full moon phase. During this phase, the sun shines fully on the side of the moon facing us for about a day. Then for the next six days, the moon's glow grows smaller on the left side because the sun is now shining on it from that direction. This is the waning gibbous phase. Waning means it is growing smaller.

During the last quarter phase, the glow covers the left half of the moon for about a day. Then, during the waning crescent phase, the glow grows smaller for six days until it disappears. The moon is then back to the new moon phase. There is no glow during this phase.

The moon phase cycle from one new moon to the next lasts about thirty days.

Extension

Find out about the Apollo program. What discoveries did astronauts make about the moon?